Working with Middle School Students

Laura P. Stowell, Ph.D.

Francisco A. Rios, Ph.D.

Janet E. McDaniel, Ph.D.

Patricia Ann Christopher, M.A.

Teacher Created Materials, Inc.

Cover Design by Darlene Spivak

Made in U.S.A.

ISBN 1-55734-888-X

Order Number TCM 888

Table of Contents

Introduction

Many have described pre-adolescence as the best of times and the worst of times. For those whose lives touch these young people, it can be equally as challenging as rewarding. However, when one is knowledgeable about what works best for young adolescents, it can be an even more rewarding experience.

"Surviving adolescence is no small matter; neither is surviving adolescents. It's a hard age to be and to teach. The worst things that ever happened to anybody happen every day. But some of the best things happen too, and they're more likely to happen when teachers understand the nature of kids and teach in ways that help students grow" (Atwell, 1987, p. 25).

We have finally come to understand that adolescence is as important a time in a person's development as infancy. Young adolescents have unique needs and interests, and the better we understand them, the better we are able to serve them and help them to grow.

The first chapter of this book lays the foundation for the book by describing who the middle school student is and what young adolescent development is all about. The second chapter discusses the evolution of the middle school and the call to change schools to meet the unique needs of these students. Chapter three is a description of the elements of effective middle schools called for in the reform reports described in chapter two. The next three chapters explore middle school curriculum, interdisciplinary teaming, and instructional practices. The last chapter describes assessment practices which are appropriate for young adolescents. Finally, there is an extensive list of resources for middle level educators.

The Early Adolescent

What they don't tell you about birthdays and what they never tell you is that when you're eleven, you're also ten, and nine, and eight, and seven, and six, and five, and four, and three, and two, and one....Like some days you may say something stupid, and that's the part of you that's still ten. Or maybe some days you might need to sit on your mama's lap because you're scared, and that's the part of you that's five....Because the way you grow old is kind of like an onion or like the rings inside a tree trunk or like my little wooden dolls that fit one inside the other, each inside the next one. That's how being eleven years old is (Cisneros, 1991, p. 6).

Early adolescence is a time of great joy but also of conflict and uncertainty

Introduction

Early adolescence is a time of great joy but also of conflict and uncertainty. It is a time when early adolescents strive for greater individual freedom while simultaneously still needing others; so, early adolescents move away from the family toward the support they believe can be found in peers. In their search for autonomy, they experiment and explore new behaviors, attitudes, and beliefs, sometimes to excess. Early adolescents strive to be different from adults while simultaneously looking to adults as role models needed for guidance and support. It is likewise a time of idealism, where actions

1

speak louder than words in pursuit of a more fair and just society.

What is never in doubt is the fact that adolescence is a time of great personal growth and change in a short time period matched only by the growth and change experienced in infancy. It differs in that the adolescent is now more aware of the growth and change he or she is experiencing (and is doing so in the company of other adolescents whose growth and change is also taking place, though at different rates) and thus is more actively thinking about it: Why is this happening and what does it mean? How will I cope with it? Why are my friends growing faster/slower than I am? How will my friends respond to my changing body/personality?

What is helpful to know is that all this change and growth experienced within an individual is influenced greatly by the people and places the adolescent is around. Growing taller is not a problem unless made so by peers or teachers who tease about one's height. Likewise, a student who risks a new way of talking about moral issues in a supportive environment can gradually come to more sophisticated ways of thinking about moral dilemmas.

Early on, adolescence was understood to be the period from just before puberty (10 years of age) to just into adulthood (18 to 20 years of age). But consider the difference between a 12-year-old and an 18-year-old; it becomes increasingly obvious that we need to be more specific about the various stages of development experienced within adolescence. Thus, it is helpful to consider adolescence as comprising three distinct sub-stages: early adolescence (10 to 14), middle adolescence (15 to 17), and late adolescence (18 to 20).

Because this book focuses on the middle school student, the focus of the material presented here will be on early adolescence. It will focus on the physical, cognitive, social, personality (with emphasis on identity), language, and moral development of early adolescence as has been described primarily by developmental psychologists. Knowledge of early adolescents' growth and development as a distinct stage with specific challenges and opportunities has been critical to the direction that middle level education reform has progressed so that the reform is informed by and responsive to the needs of early adolescence. Because early adolescence is distinct from middle adolescence or late adolescence, the kind of schooling required to be more compatible would likewise be distinct from that which typifies the high school.

> **What is never in doubt is the fact that adolescence is a time of great personal growth and change in a short time period matched only by the growth and change experienced in infancy.**

A Question of Development

Before highlighting the specific developmental characteristics and changes evident in early adolescence, several key principles are important to understand about theories of development:

◆ **Growth and development are assumed to occur in a fixed, hierarchical sequence.** This principle suggests that development progresses from one distinct stage into another distinct stage with no stages being skipped. It is hierarchical in that what happens in one stage builds on and influences what happens in later stages. The analogy of an onion, rings of a tree, or little wooden dolls described by Cisneros in the opening passage is an appropriate analogy for this principle.

◆ **Individual variation is assumed to be primarily in speed of movement between stages.** Since it is assumed that all individuals will pass through all stages in a fixed sequence, the only difference between individuals is the speed at which they progress into, through, and beyond a stage.

◆ **Individuals are never fully in one stage.** An individual moves back and forth between stages; thus, in any one time period, an individual may show signs of a previous stage, the stage he or she is in, and the stage he or she will be moving into next. While this is true, an individual tends to be in one stage most of the time for most activities. Thus, early adolescents are often looking ahead to the stage of adulthood, trying on new adult behaviors (i.e., smoking, drinking, taking control), struggling with their role in society, and concluding that there is reason to be hopeful/hopeless about society.

◆ **The individual must be understood in ways that exceed what we know about his or her development.** Although it is helpful to know about an individual's place along the developmental continuum, it is equally critical to see the individual in relation to his or her own unique values, experiences, growth rates, coping skills, knowledge base, aptitudes, etc. Thus, an early adolescent shares characteristics with other early adolescents but is different from them in important ways that must also be understood. It is these differences that make us unique individuals, and these must also be appreciated.

> The individual must be understood in ways that exceed what we know about his or her development.

3

The next section will now begin to detail some of the stages in which early adolescents find themselves in with respect to

♦ physical development
♦ cognitive development
♦ personality development
♦ social development
♦ moral development
♦ language development

While these developmental areas will be discussed separately, it should be noted that they are interrelated; that is, what is occurring in one area of development influences what occurs in another. For example, the onset of the changes that accompany puberty (physical) have implications for how the early adolescent sees him or herself (personality) and interacts with others (social). Consider that when one develops the cognitive ability to be reflective about the self and others, one can consider who he or she is, how other people feel (and thus be more mature in social relations), and develop character.

For each of these developmental areas, discussion will include the general characteristics of that stage and suggest some initial implications for teaching.

Stages of Development: Physical Development

As described earlier, the development occurring in early adolescence is as great as that experienced in infancy. Nowhere is this more true than in physical development. Consequently, the physical changes affecting early adolescents are very important to them. Individuals are achieving sexual maturity at a much younger age while there is a wider gap among youth when compared to generations past. Psychologists call this the "secular trend" (Berk, 1996).

Early adolescence is a time individuals grow in height and weight. As the individual gains weight, he or she begins the secretion of sex hormones. Emotionally, these hormones increase aggression in boys and depression in girls; they move students alternately between excitability and lethargy. Two years before puberty, in the period called pubescence, individuals begin to develop secondary sex characteristics (grow body hair, breasts, etc.). Puberty, the age at which an individual can create/bear children, begins anywhere from eight to fourteen years of age.

Two characteristics of physical development are important to consider. First, early adolescents are aware of their bodies and compare them to those of others. If they conclude that they have a positive body image, usually as exemplified by what society considers beautiful, they tend to have a positive self-image. The converse is also true about a negative body image. Second, girls mature earlier than boys and thus are dealing with their physical development earlier, especially as their growth in height and weight surpasses their male peers. As is obvious, early adolescence can be a physically uncomfortable time.

Thus, it would be helpful to plan short breaks in lessons and to provide students opportunities for movement and physical activity within the classroom environment. Equally important, students need to have opportunities to learn about and discuss the physical development that they are experiencing, to learn about the role of healthful behaviors like good sleeping and eating habits. It is true for early adolescents that good health facilitates learning and learning facilitates good health.

Stages of Development: Cognitive Development

Schools are primarily concerned with their students' cognitive development. While it is of primary consideration, it is also more difficult to describe since changes in thinking are more subtle and less observable.

Jean Piaget's work has been most widely used to describe the cognitive changes experienced in early adolescence. Piaget was primarily interested in listening and watching children as they interacted with their environment in meaningful activity. Many contemporary psychologists argue that his posture of being curious (via listening and questioning) about how children think about their world is his most important contribution—acting like Piaget is better than knowing Piaget (Duckworth, 1987).

In any event, Piaget described the changes he noted in children's thinking regarding logical-scientific reasoning (the process of forming hypotheses, testing them, and analyzing their causes and consequences). He noted that early adolescence is a time when students are moving from concrete to formal operations; that is, early adolescents are beginning to move from reasoning about real people, situations, and objects to reasoning about abstract ideas, principles, and laws. This shift, depicted in the chart on the following page is a time when the individual also becomes more self-reflective; the individual can be more aware of how he or she is thinking. It is also a time when young people come to see knowledge as relative; that is, they see knowledge as being constructed by people and being valued only to the degree that it is correct in some situations but not others.

> Schools are primarily concerned with their students' cognitive development.

5

Differences Between Concrete and Formal Operational Thinking

Characteristics of Concrete Operations	Characteristics of Formal Operations
• can solve logical problems when connected to familiar objects, actions, and observable properties	• can solve logical problems based on concepts, rules, laws, and abstract properties
• can think about multiple aspects of one object, note that its change in height does not mean it changes weight, number, volume, and classify objects in multiple ways	• can develop theories about things, deduce implications from them, consider multiple causes and consequences (even if they cannot be seen), formulate hypotheses, control variables, and test hypotheses mentally
• need step-by-step instructions if procedures are lengthy	• can plan and carry out their own (lengthy) procedure, given overall goals and resources
• are not aware of their own reasoning and therefore not critical of it; thus, do not see inconsistencies or contradictions in reasoning with outside information	• are aware of and critical of their own reasoning; check for validity of thinking by appealing to outside sources of information

(Adapted from: Messick & Reynolds, 1992)

It should be noted that early adolescents are at the beginning stages of formal operational thinking; in fact, this is a skill that will continue to develop into adulthood. While much of their day-to-day thinking is identified with concrete operations, early adolescents need opportunities to think about complex issues as they develop their abilities to reason in complex ways: to think critically, to weigh consequences, to plan solutions to problems and recognize alternative solutions, and to carry out their plans.

Piaget's Work—Important but Limited

Recall that Piaget focused only on logical/scientific reasoning. This cannot be generalized to a person's abilities to reason in other areas: physical, interpersonal, musical, verbal, and so on. For example, many persons who have not been able to perform complex, abstract reasoning on Piaget's tasks have been able to reason in complex, abstract, logical ways for everyday tasks. The ability to reason in formal operations is also influenced by literacy levels, levels of education, adaptation to Western values (since the type of logical/scientific reasoning he identified was Western oriented), nutrition, and amount of physical and social stimulation experienced.

Piaget implied that we need not be concerned with how to facilitate development; rather, he wanted us to try to understand where individuals were developmentally at the moment. It would, then, be important for teachers to pay attention to the kinds of questions students ask, how they answer teachers' questions, the strategies students use to carry out tasks, and the difficulty/ease with which they carry out those tasks (Muth & Alvermann, 1992).

> For Piaget, biological maturation and experience are critical to development.

For Piaget, biological maturation and experience are critical to development. Because early adolescents spend most of their day-to-day reasoning in concrete operations, teachers need to use a great deal of concrete examples, provide hands-on instruction, and use plenty of visuals and realia, especially when introducing new and/or complex concepts. The kinds of experiences that would be helpful include those that provide for active learning—early adolescents talking and interacting with ideas and people.

While Piaget is the best known of the developmental psychologists, the Russian psychologist Lev Vygotsky has become more prominent for the attention he applied to fostering development. Vygotsky argued that the primary means by which we grow and develop is through our interactions with others. He suggested that we first learn new ways of thinking by observing and listening to others; we then internalize what we have seen or heard, and it becomes our own. Thus for Vygotsky (1978), learning first happens interpersonally before it happens intrapsychically.

Vygotsky suggested that instruction takes place best within an individual's zone of proximal development. This is also known as ZPD or "zo-ped," the place between that which an individual already masters and that which is beyond his or her ability. The ZPD is the area where a student can function capably, given the support, guidance, encouragement, and mentorship of more capable others. Thus, while Piaget would ask that we be sensitive to and teach at the level

7

students are at, Vygotsky would ask that we lead early adolescents to the next stage of development by providing them with more complex, abstract ideas and problems while simultaneously providing access to the guidance and encouragement that others who are more expert can give.

Teachers should, according to Vygotskian psychology, provide challenging activities that are within early adolescents' zones of proximal development. In doing so, the teacher needs to attend to the kind of support and guidance that can be provided so that the student can be successful, given the task and the guidance. Heterogeneous cooperative group activities would also serve well in this regard (Forman, Minick, & Stone, 1993; Muth & Alvermann, 1992).

Stages of Development: Personality Development

As was noted about early adolescents' cognitive development, the ability to reflect on the self is growing during this time period. This leads many to misinterpret early adolescence as a time of egocentrism similar to that of infancy. While it is true that early adolescents are more self-conscious and introspective, it differs in that they are considering what they believe others are thinking about them. In other words, they perceive that there is an imaginary audience and they are the actors. This accounts for much of the perceived egocentrism.

Early adolescence is a time when students are, in their reflection, concerned with finding themselves (their identity/self-concept), evaluating their perceived abilities/skills, and developing positive or negative feelings about those identities and/or abilities (levels of self-esteem). Note that a person's perception of the self includes the many aspects of self: the social self, the academic self, the athletic self, the physical self, the moral self, the ideological self, etc. Some of these selves are more important than others. For early adolescents, the selves of dominant importance are the social, physical, and sexual/gender selves. In later adolescence they become more concerned with their vocational and moral identities.

Erik Erickson has had much to say about personality development, and his theory of psychological and social development spans from birth to death. He argued that the major task for early adolescents was to struggle between role confusion and identity, to become aware of who they are and whether this picture of the self is consistent with the images others have of them. They are keenly aware of and seek the judgments of their peers and adults whose opinions they value.

For early adolescents, the selves of dominant importance are the social, physical, and sexual/gender selves.

James Marcia (1980) was primarily concerned with occupational identity and extended Erickson's model, based on the principles that people have to make a commitment to some identity, that forming an identity requires a time for exploration, and that students move from a variety of stages in search of answering the question, "Who am I?" Marcia suggested that students move from a stage where identity is not considered at all (identity diffusion) to a stage where they explore their identity (identity moratorium) on their way to identity achievement. Often, students will stay in the moratorium stage, looking to find who they are but committing to no specific identity, and sometimes students will adopt an identity too soon, without exploring other, more appropriate alternatives, which he called identity foreclosure.

Recall that students in middle schools are primarily concerned with their physical appearance, with coming to terms with what it means to be masculine/feminine, with being recognized by those who count, and with beginning to consider where they are going. Thus, teachers will do well to give students vicarious experiences like books, videos, and poetry by and about other early adolescents undergoing the identity challenge. Teachers might also discuss with students aspects of masculinity and femininity that are positive and productive and encourage all students to adapt those traits. To help them get the recognition they need from social networks, early adolescents should be taught social skills. An excellent book of activities on this for middle level students is *Skill-Streaming the Adolescent* (Goldstein, 1980). Finally, to help them consider where they are going, the teacher might consider having students role play a variety of roles, do value clarification exercises, and identify for themselves some short-term goals. Teaching students about identity development itself also helps provide early adolescents with a framework for understanding their world.

> **Teaching students about identity development itself also helps provide early adolescents with a framework for understanding their world.**

A Note About Gender and Race

Gilligan (1982) has argued that the notion of an identity search for self in one's occupation is primarily a masculine concept. She argues that females tend to develop their identity through their relationships with others with a heavy focus on intimacy and significant relationships. She suggests that seeking a balance between occupational and relational identities is healthy for all students.

Students of color are placed in a unique role since they are concerned about what their racial/cultural background means with respect to their identities. This is made significant if the students come to see themselves as different from the mainstream, especially when their race/ethnicity is not accepted, appreciated, or understood. Thus, early adolescent students of color have to choose to assimilate (deny their racial/ethnic background and thereby become "white") and identify most with the dominant group only, integrate and identify with both groups, separate and only identify with their home group, or become marginalized by not being able to identify with any group, and thereby become "raceless." It should be noted that a recent study found that students who integrated had the most positive levels of psychological development and self-esteem, academic achievement, and care for others different from themselves; those students who assimilated had decreased levels of self-esteem (Phinney, Chavira, & Williamson, 1992). As might be imagined, early adolescents from biracial backgrounds also have a difficult time with these issues.

Issues of ethnic identity are magnified for students who are high achievers since achieving is often thought of as "selling out" and "acting white." Thus, many high achievers are forced to either hide their achievements, underachieve, or become raceless—empty the self of their race.

> They still recognize the power of strong, sustained guidance from adults.

All this is not to suggest that ethnic identity issues are strictly for "minorities." More recent research has focused on the stages Euro-American students go through in coming to terms with being "white," especially those associated with recognizing their own ethnicity and the privileges that come with it, overcoming racism, and dealing with the negative feelings associated with contemporary and historical injustices brought on by whites against communities of color (Tatum, 1992).

Ethnic identity, like any other type of identity, will not resolve itself automatically. It requires teachers to undertake some interventions to push students along in this regard. Again, vicarious experiences about students dealing with their ethnicity, role playing where students are asked to assume ethnic roles different from their own, seeking to make a place for the voice of the experience of ethnic minority communities, and opportunities for students to discuss social issues will all be productive in helping move students toward positive resolutions of these challenges.

Stages of Development: Social Development

Closely related to personality development is social development. As suggested in the introduction of this chapter, early adolescents are seeking independence from their families, though they continue to care about what their family thinks and strive to reconsider how the child-adult relationship might proceed. They seek to make friendships with new adults. They still recognize the power of strong, sustained guidance from adults. They are also concerned with making close, personal friendships with peers. Early adolescents want to be respected, valued, and connected to positive groups of their peers.

Early adolescence is a time when students are capable of being aware of their own perspectives and being aware of the perspectives of another (making personal relationships possible) but also of being aware of generic "others." Thus, they will consider not only their own thoughts about a relationship but also the thoughts of the other person and of how other teens think about that relationship. It is critical to note that this generic other is usually someone to whom the teen can relate, such as another teen. Thus, peer groups are very important to early adolescents; these groups apply considerable pressure to conform, are difficult to become part of, and have a clear order of status within the group.

During early adolescence, students begin to consider how generic others unlike themselves, like adults or people from different cultural/linguistic backgrounds, might consider things. This perspective-taking ability is critical since understanding how others, both those we know personally and those we do not, feel and think is critical to our developing empathy, care, respect, and kindness. Those who cannot take the perspective of others tend to be able to do harmful acts and feel no remorse or guilt (MacQuiddy, Maise, & Hamilton, 1987).

To foster social development, early adolescents would be well served by being taught social skills, by being required to role play and take on the perspectives of those both like them and different from them, by being given the opportunities to interact with a variety of people (including adults), and by being given some decision-making control to help them develop a sense of responsibility.

Briefly, early adolescents are at a stage where moral issues become critical as they consider, reflect, discuss, and debate big social issues.

Stages of Development: Moral Development

Briefly, early adolescents are at a stage where moral issues become critical as they consider, reflect, discuss, and debate big social issues. Kohlberg suggested that early adolescents are between stage two (doing what they think is right based on what they will be rewarded by others for doing) and stage three (doing what pleases others) as they move toward stage four (doing what is right based on following the rules and preserving the social order). But it is also a time where early adolescents are idealistic in their values and attitudes, developing a sense of fairness wherein they are eager to point out the contradictions they see in the ideal and the real. It is a time when they are interested in finding just, positive alternatives to racism, sexism, and prejudice, especially when they have the opportunity to form close friendships with those who differ from them (Manning, 1994).

Early adolescents need teachers who are clear about the rules established for appropriate behavior in a classroom, the reasons for those rules, and the fair application of those rules with consistent follow-up. Again, early adolescents benefit from goal-setting opportunities, value clarifications, opportunities to make choices, and being responsible for their actions to others in the classroom. Beyond the classroom, a sense of social responsibility can be enhanced by way of community activity best exemplified by service learning.

Stages of Development: Language Development

It is difficult to capture the complexity of what teachers need to know about language development centered around early adolescents who either speak no English (NEP) or are limited in their English language ability (LEP). Yet, early adolescents who are NEP also go to middle schools. We would encourage the reader to consider more comprehensive training in this area than can be provided here. (As a start, see California State Department of Education, 1991; Diaz-Rico & Weed, 1995; Garcia, 1994; and Lessow-Hurley, 1990). However, to begin the process, consider the following principles upon which bilingual education and second language acquisition theory resides.

Beyond the classroom, a sense of social responsibility can be enhanced by way of community activity best exemplified by service learning.

- ◆ Students learn a second language in much the same way they learned their first language: a silent period, one-word answers, simple sentences, complex sentences, fluency.

- ◆ The amount of time it takes to learn a second language mirrors that of the first language: two years for basic interpersonal communication (BICS) and five to seven years for cognitive, academic communication (CALPS) that is used in classrooms.

- ◆ Proficiency in one's first language facilitates learning in the second language since there is a common underlying proficiency between languages (CUPS).

- ◆ NEP and LEP early adolescents in middle schools need to become proficient in both academic content and the English language.

- ◆ Bilingual education is positive because of the following reasons: it helps teach students content while they are learning English, there are CUPS between languages, it enhances student self-esteem which is also critical to academic success, and it pushes students to become fully proficient in the primary language. Full proficiency in two languages leads to greater cognitive flexibility, metalinguistic awareness, concept formation, divergent thinking, and creativity among other benefits.

◆ Instruction by English-only middle school teachers of LEP students is enhanced when the grade appropriate content is made comprehensible via pictures, simplified speech, realia, and content connected to student experience in a classroom environment that is supportive and comfortable for these students.

An Alternative Perspective

While this chapter has focused on the developmental trends observed in Western culture, it has been noted by anthropologists that no such distinct stages seem to occur in other (non-Western) cultures. Thus, many anthropologists reject these developmental stages as universal. What accounts for this apparent lack of recognition of stages of adolescence? It is believed that non-Western cultures are structured so that there is greater continuity between childhood and adulthood. Consider the following:

> **Recall that development is taking place within an individual, but how it is experienced is greatly influenced by people and institutions.**

◆ We strive to teach early adolescents to take on an adult role that is different from the role they played in childhood, while in many non-Western cultures, the adult role evolves out of the roles learned as children.

◆ We strive to teach early adolescents to take on responsibility associated with adulthood while in many non-Western cultures individuals are given much responsibility in childhood and so learn responsibility early on.

◆ We strive to teach early adolescents to suppress their sexual feelings until adulthood, at which point they are supposed to be able to release them, while in many non-Western cultures sexual feelings are not suppressed, except for the universal taboo against incest.

Thus, it is critical to recognize that the notion of distinct stages of development during early adolescence comes from the discontinuous experience of childhood and adulthood early adolescents experience in Western cultures (Rice, 1995).

Concluding Remarks

Having reviewed what we know about the developmental changes that early adolescents are experiencing generally, the implications for teaching and schooling in middle level grades becomes clearer. There are implications for the curriculum, teaching, and schooling. Recall that development is taking place within an individual, but how it is experienced is greatly influenced by people and institutions.

With respect to curriculum and teaching, it is clear that students need to think about things like content, especially when that content is meaningful to their lives. Teaching students higher order thinking skills unconnected to an academic area such as history, mathematics, or science is not as helpful as when they are taught in relation to meaningful content. One suggestion is to provide a task-focused environment (Urdan, Midgley, and Wood, 1995).

With respect to schooling, it is clear that students need to interact with caring adults in school, and community institutions like churches and community centers that understand and meet the developmental concerns of early adolescents.

And, most of all it is clear that the curriculum, instruction, teachers, caregivers, schools, and other community institutions need to work in concert. Since the developmental needs of early adolescents are interdependent, it is likewise critical for the people and organizations responsible for helping them to act interdependently.

> Early adolescence is a time when positive interventions can make a difference.

Early adolescence is a time when positive interventions can make a difference. But it is also a time when failure to make a difference comes at a powerful cost: personally, resulting in an individual who feels alienation, hatred, and rage; and socially, resulting in illiteracy, crime, violence, disease, disability, and ignorance.

What happens to an individual during early adolescence really matters. The behavior patterns established tend to be sustained into adulthood. Early adolescence is a time when individuals become hopeful about their futures and act positively to make a difference, or become hopeless and act negatively in response to their anger and depression. They learn how to cultivate relationships and see the power of positive role models, or they end up crushing relationships and become influenced by negative role models. They learn that school is meaningful and, thus, a worthwhile endeavor, or they push away from it as unconnected and unimportant to their lives. It is therefore critical that caring adults, especially teachers, make strong connections to young adolescents.

Why Middle School?

Middle School Reform Movement

It is the nature of schools to adapt to meet the needs of their clientele as new information is gained about that clientele. Middle level education is no different. As new insights were gained about the development of the young adolescent, schools attempted to institute changes. These changes came from a number of sources and for a variety of reasons, and are depicted on the following page. The junior high school caught on and spread after 1918. In 1920, one of every five high school graduates had attended two schools—grades one through eight and nine through twelve. By 1960, four out of every five high school graduates had attended three schools—grades one through six, seven through nine, and ten through twelve. The junior high had become common. However, by 1973, a middle school movement was building momentum due to dissatisfaction with the junior high school configuration and philosophy. Middle schools have grown in the past two decades, while the number of junior highs has decreased. By 1993, there were approximately three middle schools for every junior high. The most current statistics (National Department of Education, 1995) show that in 1993–1994 the total number of schools serving grades five through nine was 13,543 compared to 10,395 in 1970.

> As new insights were gained about the development of the young adolescent, schools attempted to institute changes.

Course of Middle Level Education in the United States

Group/Individual Proposing	Change Proposed	Date	Reasons
Cardinal principles of secondary education	Elementary school include the first six years and divide the high school period into two sections—junior and senior	1918	• Large number of immigrants needing to be "Americanized" • Concern for dropout rate, especially before grade nine • Start college preparation earlier
Florida Department of Supervision and Curriculum Development of the Florida Education Association	Recommend experimentation with different approaches for this age group	1954	• Dissatisfaction with the junior high
James Conant, President of Harvard University, Report on High Schools with special set of recommendations for junior high	Group students by ability	1959	• National pressures to compete in the space race (Sputnik) • Most junior high teachers trained to be high school teachers and so junior highs tended to look like high schools
William Alexander, Donald Eichhorn, Paul George, John Lounsbury, and Gordon Vars founded the National Middle School Association	Early adolescents should have a distinctive program and started promoting the use of the title Middle School	1973	• Conflicting professional views and public pressure about the purposes of intermediate schooling • New studies of the earlier maturation of children
A Nation at Risk	More academic rigor Increase test scores	1983	• Growing concern over the world status of the United States, i.e., trade balance, growing national debt, economic decline, advancing technology, and so attention turned to the quality of schools
School based studies: *Caught in the Middle: Educational Reform for Young Adolescents in California Public Schools* (State) *Turning Points* (National)	Adhere to middle school philosophy while pushing for greater academic excellence	1987 1989	• "Back to basics" movement • Response to public concern over national reports

Middle School Reform Documents

Middle level reform has been guided by scholarly research and the principles outlined in a number of private and government sponsored documents. The late 1980s publications of *Caught in the Middle: Educational Reform for Young Adolescents in California Public Schools* (Middle Grades Task Force, 1987) and *Turning Points: Preparing American Youth for the 21st Century* (Carnegie Council on Adolescent Development, 1989) set the agenda for middle level reform. *Turning Points* provides the most succinct statement of principles in its eight recommendations for middle level education:

◆ Create small communities for learning where stable, close, mutually respectful relationships with adults and peers are considered fundamental for intellectual development and personal growth.

◆ Teach a core academic program.

◆ Ensure success for all students through flexibility in arranging instructional time, adequate resources for teachers, and the elimination of tracking by achievement level.

◆ Empower teachers and administrators to make decisions about the experiences of middle grade students.

◆ Staff middle grade schools with teachers who are experts at teaching young adolescents.

◆ Improve academic performance through fostering the health and fitness of young adolescents.

◆ Reengage families in the education of young adolescents.

◆ Connect schools with communities which together share the responsibility for each middle grade student's success.

> Middle level reform has been guided by scholarly research and the principles outlined in a number of private and government sponsored documents.

The elaboration and implementation of these principles is a major purpose of the National Middle School Association (NMSA), established in 1977. In *This We Believe* (1995), the association issued a "call for action" to restructure schools for young adolescents. They claimed developmentally responsive middle schools are characterized by the following:

◆ educators knowledgeable about and committed to young adolescents

◆ shared vision

◆ high expectations for all

- an adult advocate for every student
- family and community partnerships
- a positive school climate

If a school meets these characteristics, then it will provide:

- curriculum that is challenging, integrative, and exploratory
- varied teaching and learning approaches
- assessment and evaluation procedures that promote learning
- flexible organizational structures
- programs and policies that foster health, wellness, and safety
- comprehensive guidance and support services

In the 1990s, a sharp increase in the quality and quantity of practical resources elaborated the principles set forth by the calls for reform in the 1980s. See the reference section for a more complete list of these resources.

More recently, *Great Transitions: Preparing Adolescents for a New Century* (1995), the concluding report of the Carnegie Council on Adolescent Development, was filed. This report reemphasizes its core recommendations, identifies new risks facing ten-to-fourteen-year-olds, and discusses what other institutions besides schools, such as business, government, and scientific and professional organizations, can do for young adolescents.

In the years between *Turning Points* and *Great Transitions*, studies have begun on the effects of these recommendations and middle schools on young adolescents. *Great Transitions* reports on one comprehensive study. A group of middle schools in Illinois which implemented the *Turning Points* recommendations has been studied since 1991. Results thus far show that in forty-two schools participating, the implementation of the *Turning Points* recommendations is associated with significant improvement in students' reading, mathematics, and language arts achievement. In addition, teachers' and students' ratings show that as the recommendations are implemented, "students in these schools are less likely to feel alienated, fearful, or depressed in school and more likely to have high self-esteem" (Carnegie Council on Adolescent Development, 1995, p. 88).

Differences Among Elementary, Middle, and High Schools

The middle school experience is different from the elementary or high school but not so severely different that the transition is difficult. The elements of the exemplary middle school are designed to meet the needs of the young adolescent but also to provide a smooth transition from elementary school through middle school to high school. Rather than self-contained as in the elementary school or segmented as in the high school, the middle school is configured into interdisciplinary teams or villages in which students are part of a smaller group within the larger grade or school group. Classes are blocked together so that students do not have as many teachers or class periods as they do in high school but more than they did in elementary. The schedule is often more flexible than that of a high school, and on some days resembles the large blocks of time in one room which typifies the elementary school schedule. The middle school curriculum builds on and extends the skills learned in the elementary grades and is more exploratory and broader in nature than the narrower and deeper focus of the high school curriculum. The grouping of students is also more flexible. Rather than group students strictly chronologically as in the elementary setting or strictly by disciplines (and often by ability) as in the high school, classes can be heterogeneous and multi-aged.

The grouping of students is also more flexible.

Differences Between Junior High and Middle Schools

As indicated earlier, the junior high school concept really spread after 1918. The increased birth rate following World War I and the increase in immigration led to overcrowded schools. One answer to this was to move students grades seven through nine to a new building.

The middle school usually includes grades six through eight or five through eight and sometimes seven through eight. Junior highs were usually grades seven through nine. The junior high was not thought of as serving a distinctly different function from the high school or even the elementary school. Many attribute the evolution of the junior high to a dissatisfaction with the two-level grouping of grades one through eight and nine through twelve. Common differences between junior high schools and middle schools are noted on the following page.

	Junior High School	Middle School
Student-Teacher relationship	Random contact	Teacher-advisor
Student grouping	Homogeneous/Subject	Heterogeneous/Multi-age
Curriculum	Separated	Integrated
Building organization	Departments	Team, Village, House
Schedule	Periods, Exploratory, & Electives	Block Scheduling/Flexible
Sports, Arts, Clubs	Competitive by ability	Inclusive, noncompetitive
Teacher preparation	Academic specialist	Balance between students and academics

Concluding Remarks

The middle school movement has been called "the green and growing edge of American education." It is the vanguard of educational reform. Many changes have taken place "in the middle." Restructuring middle schools has become the most influential and successful educational reform movement of this century. The importance of creating developmentally responsive middle level schools cannot be underestimated. "The nature of educational programs young adolescents experience during this formative period will in large measure determine our future" (National Middle School Association, 1995, p. 1). How can schools respond to this challenge?

Elements of a Middle School

The Vision

The vision of a developmentally responsive middle school that meets the needs of young adolescents is a lofty one—but one that is worth the effort it will take to achieve. Traditionally, middle level schools have not been effective in meeting the needs of young adolescents. They have neglected their own clients, treating them either as bigger children or smaller adolescents. They have been equipped with buildings, staff, and materials that were hand-me-downs from other levels of schooling. Until the middle school movement of recent years, schools for young adolescents have been more like holding tanks than centers of learning. In lessons learned from the successes of the middle school movement, educators now have a well-formed idea of the essentials of successful schools for young adolescents. This chapter presents brief sketches of several of the agreed-upon elements that make up a model middle school. These elements are educators committed to young adolescents, a balanced core curriculum, interdisciplinary teaming, organization of time and space, instructional practices, advisory programs, exploratory programs, and connections between the school, the home, and the community.

> Traditionally, middle level schools have not been effective in meeting the needs of young adolescents.

21

Educators Committed to Young Adolescents

Educational reform documents targeting early adolescents suggest a radical departure from the way the junior high school is currently operating. If these reforms are to take hold, teachers must be informed about these changes, as well as be prepared to relate and teach effectively the children with whom they work. In *This We Believe* (1995), the National Middle School Association proposes that middle level teachers possess a genuine desire to work with and teach middle students. In the past, junior high teachers had their sights set on teaching at the high school level. They accepted junior high teaching positions because of their availability. While it is true that many of these teachers came to appreciate and even prefer teaching the middle school child, they remained largely untrained in effective middle level teaching and learning. Resistance to middle level reform has been due in part to these teachers protesting any changes that would make their middle level school less like a traditional high school. Beyond the desire to teach middle grade students, "wise and experienced" middle level teachers must understand several components of their work (McEwin, Dickinson, Erb, & Scales, 1995). These components are young adolescent development, middle grades curriculum, middle grades instruction, middle grades school organization, family and community relations, and middle grades teaching roles. Few middle level schools are staffed entirely with these teachers. However, with a commitment to both initial and career-long professional preparation by those who teach young adolescents, the vision of such a staff can come closer to being a reality.

> It seems that a natural place to begin educating teachers about the middle school student and middle level teaching is during the teacher preparation program.

Preservice Teachers

It seems that a natural place to begin educating teachers about the middle school student and middle level teaching is during the teacher preparation program. A program specifically designed for middle school teachers would be most effective in preparing these teachers to take on the challenges of teaching at a middle school. Despite the need for middle grades preservice preparation, a distinct minority of middle grades teachers—about 17% in a 1991 study—have received such preparation (Scales, 1992). Ideally, middle grades preservice programs would recruit candidates who have the desire to be with young adolescents and then provide them with a thorough understanding of foundational studies such as young child development, diversity, technology, interpersonal communication, classroom management, family connections, and school reform. Specialized knowledge about middle schooling is also necessary—for example, young adolescent development, middle school organization, teacher roles and the curriculum, teaching and learning that are developmentally appropriate (McEwin, et al. 1995). The importance of knowledge and appreciation of diversity in its many forms, race, ethnicity, language, exceptionalities, and so on, is particularly important for middle grades teachers. Given what we know about identity formation of the young adolescent, it becomes imperative that new teachers understand effective ways of reaching all children. Middle grades teachers should have preparation in at least two content areas so that they are able to teach in a block schedule like language arts and social studies or mathematics and science. This also helps them see connections to multiple disciplines should they work in an interdisciplinary team. Finally, middle grades preparation programs benefit from being offered on a middle school site so that the prospective teachers are in the thick of things while they are building knowledge and a commitment to teaching young adolescents.

Inservice Training

Recruiting new teachers who have a desire and are skilled in working with the middle school child is certainly one way to reform middle schools; however, what about existing teachers on a school site? First and foremost, the principal and other site administrators need to be well informed on the rationale for and research that supports middle level reform. An early step toward participatory reform is the collaborative development and clear communication of a vision. When teachers, parents, students, and community leaders form a consensus around middle level reform, the chances of success are much greater. The enthusiasm and commitment of experienced teachers is crucial in this effort. Many middle level teachers choose to take university courses that focus on teaching and learning in middle schools; about 33% of teachers surveyed in five states indicated they had pursued such graduate coursework (McEwin, Dickinson, Erb, & Scales, 1995).

Middle level reform, like any systematic change, takes time and sometimes includes painful episodes.

Middle level reform, like any systematic change, takes time and sometimes includes painful episodes. A good place to begin is with teacher inservice about the reform movement and the growth and development of young adolescents. As teachers begin to understand and appreciate the power of reform elements, they may want to try one aspect of the reform early on. For instance, three or four teachers may want to form an interdisciplinary team. Site administrators need to be supportive—emotionally and financially—for this type of risk-taking behavior. Likewise, administrators need to be willing to reassign teachers to other schools or grade levels if the teachers prefer not to be involved with the middle level reform.

A Balanced Core Curriculum

All middle school students should receive a common, academically rigorous curriculum that provides a foundation of knowledge and skills essential for success at higher grade levels and in preparation for life. Such a curriculum should provide a balance between academic, social, personal, and vocational goals.

Core curriculum in the middle grades makes a good deal of sense. The notion has been around for a long time (Vars, 1961). Why is it then that all children are not receiving a core curriculum? Students whose primary language is other than English have perhaps the most difficult time consistently receiving the same curriculum as native English speakers. This may be due to staffing difficulties and finding teachers who speak the primary language of the English learner. Translating materials and locating adequate resources in the native language compound the problem. These children may go years without receiving the full complement of subjects provided to the native English speaker. Even when they do attend a class with the same subject title, the curriculum is often watered down. This lack of equity is not easy to remedy. Finding qualified staff requires a dogged commitment to solving the problem. It also requires that the school site or district offer professional development opportunities to teach monolingual teachers effective strategies for teaching English learners. This type of instruction, often called "sheltered instruction," assists English learners by providing comprehensible input for the acquisition of appropriate grade level knowledge and skills as they emerge into greater English proficiency.

> **Unfortunately, due to a lack of common planning time for teachers, the curriculum is often splintered and/or repetitive.**

Often students in special education classes face a similar problem. The issue is not based on language concerns but rather on a belief that students receiving special education assistance cannot handle the rigors of an adopted core curriculum. While it is true that due to learning handicaps, students might have difficulty reading certain pieces of literature on their own or writing lengthy essays without assistance, there are a myriad of ways to present information and assess learning that involves these students actively in the core curriculum.

Also affected are children who are tracked into slower classes. The curriculum is not only dumbed down, but often the teaching strategies encourage passive participation of the students, with a reliance on simple recall questions and responses.

But what of students in the average or advanced classes? Are they consistently receiving a standard, core curriculum? Unfortunately, due to a lack of common planning time for teachers, the curriculum is often splintered and/or repetitive. Also, scheduling issues keep students from experiencing the full course of recommended subjects.

An excellent remedy for this problem is the notion of the interdisciplinary team structure, the subject of chapter four. Untracking a middle school also opens up scheduling possibilities so students are guaranteed a full complement of courses. Perhaps the surest way of making the core curriculum a reality for all students is for teachers and administrators to realize the necessity of providing such a curriculum to all children and, at the same time, for teachers to broaden their teaching repertoires to include strategies and techniques that will achieve the goals of the core curriculum.

Teams of Teachers

The thought of teachers working together in groups or teams is not a new idea. However, the middle school reform movement elevated this notion by ascribing many positive benefits to teaming, both for students and the teachers on the team. Collaborative work in non-instructional areas has long been common in schools. For example, teachers work together in subject area departments, in faculty governance sub-committees, or as members of student guidance teams. Teachers and students often work together in sports competitions, student governance, and extracurricular activities or clubs. Nonetheless, teachers and students working collaboratively to pursue academic goals, coordinate curriculum, and develop skills is a new way to think of a team. The middle level reform documents call this the interdisciplinary team organization.

Probably the most important component of the interdisciplinary team is the sharing of students by several teachers who are responsible for most or all of the students' classes.

Probably the most important component of the interdisciplinary team is the sharing of students by several teachers who are responsible for most or all of the students' classes. The most effective teams meet together very often. A common planning period facilitates this situation. The teaming classrooms should also be physically close together. A well-organized team becomes, in effect, a school-within-a-school organization, where teachers and students have autonomy to create a learning environment that is most responsive to students' needs.

While the structure of interdisciplinary teams can take many forms, most often the curriculum being taught is carefully planned by the teachers, usually with suggestions from students on the team. The curriculum is integrated across subject areas. Repetition between classes is reduced, and common concepts and skills are emphasized. Effective teams coordinate classroom rules and procedures, grading policies, and tools of assessment. A team identity is developed over time through choosing a name, adopting a uniform (a team shirt, for example), fielding intramural sports teams, and holding activities such as field trips or after-school games. The team becomes a "home base" for students and teachers—a caring environment within the all too often impersonal atmosphere of a large school with hundreds of students. Interdisciplinary team organization is examined in more detail in chapter four.

Organization of Time and Space

Many educational leaders believe that effective scheduling is the most important element of an exemplary middle school (George & Alexander, 1993). The traditional junior high schedule mirrors that of a high school, with six or seven distinct periods of instruction. This structure makes it unlikely that a student will experience a coherent curriculum in any given day. A likely scenario is that a mathematics test is followed by an English essay on Mark Twain, followed by a volleyball game, and then, by a video on ocean currents. By the end of seven periods of this routine, day after day, it is no wonder that a 13-year-old student retains less content knowledge and fewer skills than all his well-intentioned teachers would like.

It is critical that teachers on the team have a common planning time, as well.

A developmentally responsive middle school schedule reflects the school vision and keeps yearly priorities in mind as new approaches to time and space are considered. Above all, the schedule is designed to be responsive to—not destructive to—the cognitive, physical, and social development of the young adolescents who actually live the schedule. Some considerations to think about when planning a middle school master schedule include:

◆ Think about the schedules of the sixth, seventh, and eighth grade students. All students should have the same autonomy as to course selection. Do they have the same number of teachers? Are multi-age classes offered for all students?

◆ Are there interdisciplinary teams? If so, some extended blocks of instructional time need to be incorporated into the schedule. It is critical that teachers on the team have a common planning time, as well.

◆ How are exploratory classes structured? How often do classes meet? Is there a balance among the types of exploratory classes students will be taking throughout the grades?

◆ When does the advisory class meet? Does it meet for a longer period of time on certain days for a special activity? Do students have access to other guidance activities and tutorials?

◆ Do all students have equal access to instructional programs? For example, if a student needs to take English as a Second Language, is he or she still able to take seventh grade science?

- ◆ Are subject areas appropriately taught in a two or three-period block (e.g., language arts/social studies or mathematics/science) and accommodated in the schedule?

- ◆ Is it possible to vary the schedule during the week so that some days the students experience a full array of courses, but on other days fewer but longer class periods are held? Or, would all the teachers prefer meeting their classes for longer class periods (say sixty to seventy minutes), so that a seven-period cycle takes more than one day to accomplish? Perhaps not all classes need to meet for the same number of minutes each day. What is to be gained or lost by designing longer periods with less frequency?

- ◆ Should a modified schedule be established for special activity days, assembly days, or testing?

Schools involved in middle level reform are experimenting with innovative schedule variations. If an interdisciplinary team is scheduled for the first five periods of the day as a self-contained entity, then that team can create its own schedule from week to week. For instance, one week social studies might need to meet for two hours each day and then for the next week meet less frequently.

Schools involved in middle level reform are experimenting with innovative schedule variations.

Some schools have created a block schedule where classes meet for two periods on certain days of the week. This permits teachers to plan extended lessons or activities that cannot be completed in a fifty-minute period.

Creating an effective and instructionally responsive schedule is one of the most cognitively demanding activities of a school staff. Due to constraints of time, money, and faculty support, it is seldom that any one schedule facilitates all the middle school reform elements. It then becomes imperative that schools prioritize their goals for that year and see that they are reflected in the schedule.

Finally, developing a master schedule should be a collaborative effort, a "consensus among staff, students and parents" (Middle Grades Task Force, 1987). Also, any schedule should be considered dynamic, alterable, and reflective of the changing needs of the students and faculty.

Instructional Practices

After examining the growth and development of the ten to fourteen-year-old, there remains little doubt that in order to be responsive to the physical, cognitive, social, and emotional demands of the age, instructional practices must be varied. Teaching strategies and techniques must also reflect the needs of the subjects studied as part of the middle school curriculum. Instructional strategies appropriate for young adolescents are examined in chapter six, Instructional Practices.

Exploratory Courses

Of all of the recommendations for middle level reform, exploration alone has its roots in the junior high reform movement in the 1940s. The rationale for exploratory classes was almost the same then as it is today. That is, young adolescence is a time for tremendous growth of personal interests. What better way to expose young people to all that life has to offer in terms of hobbies, fine arts, music, and careers than to offer elective or exploratory classes. Also, there is a close relationship between exploratory curriculum and increased student skill development (George & Lawrence, 1982).

In junior high schools, exploratory classes were almost always limited to electives in fine arts, home economics, industrial arts, and music.

In junior high schools, exploratory classes were almost always limited to electives in fine arts, home economics, industrial arts, and music. Only since the advent of middle level reform has exploration taken on a much broader definition. There are multiple ways to organize exploratory programs; these are discussed in the next chapter.

Extracurricular Activities

Following the same rationale for exploratory classes, providing adolescent youngsters with a variety of extracurricular activities is considered another important element of an exemplary middle school. Extracurricular activities can take the form of clubs or intramurals. These activities should be open to all youngsters and serve to broaden their interests and, at the same time, give them a sense of belonging to the larger school community. Extracurricular activities can occur before school, during recess or lunch, or after school. However, serious consideration must be given to providing equal access for all students. For example, if students usually take the bus home or live a long distance from the school, these extracurricular activities are best planned during lunch so more students can participate. Extracurricular activities can also help positively connect students and teachers outside of the classroom.

Clubs

Clubs can be about anything that students and teachers are interested in. Sometimes established organizations come on campus, such as Boy Scouts or Girl Scouts, 4-H clubs, junior Kiwanis, or Rotary clubs. Students at this age are also interested in service learning projects where they go out into the community to help in some way.

Intramurals

During middle grades, students are still discovering what sport activities they like to participate in and how it feels to be a member of a team. Intramural sports are an excellent way to foster this discovery process. As opposed to the competitive, interscholastic team sports played in high schools, middle school intramurals are open to all students, boys and girls alike, with no "cuts" due to skill level. Too, the trappings of high school sports, including cheerleaders, are to be avoided. Often, intramural games are played between advisory classrooms or interdisciplinary teams. The emphasis of intramurals is inclusiveness, team spirit, and camaraderie.

Advisory

Throughout a child's life, but especially during early adolescence, it is essential for young people to see positive and effective examples of interpersonal communication. Given cuts in funding of guidance personnel and the fact that middle school students are no longer with only one teacher throughout the day, it is imperative that every student have an adult advocate in the school. This reasoning has given rise to advisory programs. While advisory takes many forms, it was originally conceived so that all adults in the school would advise a small group of students. Since all adults would be involved—teachers, administrators, secretaries, custodians, counselors, librarians, and other personnel—the number of students in a group would be fewer than the average academic class size. In this conception, advisory groups meet every day for fifteen to twenty minutes. Stevenson (1992) suggests that the groups meet one additional afternoon each week for thirty to forty minutes.

> While advisory takes many forms, it was originally conceived so that all adults in the school would advise a small group of students.

The Advisor

The primary responsibility of the advisor is to build a nonacademic relationship with students, one in which the students see that they are appreciated and cared for by school adults outside of the classroom setting. While this usually occurs over a one-year period, some schools are experimenting with an advisor staying with a group for three years (sixth, seventh, and eighth grades). Another responsibility of the advisor is to become well acquainted with the students' academic performances. In many cases, the advisor is the first adult to notice when a student's performance changes—when evidence such as progress reports and discipline referrals from teachers begin to show a change. The advisor attends parent conferences and other meetings involving advisees. If the interest was solely academic, the advisory concept would not be nearly so powerful, but due to the activities that occur in advisory period and the personal conferences, the advisor comes to understand and know the child personally. Often the advisor builds a lasting relationship with the advisee and his or her parents. The advisor acts as an advocate for the student to other teachers.

The Advisory Period

The advisory period is usually a time where general housekeeping activities occur. In many schools, advisory is the first period of the day when attendance and lunch count are taken. Often, this is also a time where teachers check to make sure students have completed their homework.

Many schools have adopted a curriculum for advisory. This curriculum usually consists of short activities that work on developing self-esteem and responsibility. Often study skills is a topic in the advisory curriculum. One hallmark of effective advisory classes is active student participation in meaningful discussions. There is usually a time for special recognition on occasions such as birthdays and honor awards. Some very successful advisory classes are involved in service projects in and out of school.

In order for advisory to be successful, there needs to be adequate teacher support and commitment. Sometimes teachers are not comfortable with students on a personal level. Training in communication skills and group facilitation is helpful for advisors. The school counselor can provide assistance and support for teachers who lack confidence in this area.

Benefits of Advisory

Schools with an active advisory program report a decline in discipline problems on campus. Students benefit from personal contact with an adult, and they see the advisory program as a place where the democratic process can occur easily. Once parents are made aware of the program, they are generally supportive and report more positive feelings toward the school. Teachers also report many positive personal benefits from advisory. They appreciate really coming to know a group of students and feel less isolated themselves.

Counselors

Even the best advisory program will not take the place of professional middle school counselors. While advisory can often provide a forum for dealing with relatively minor school or personal problems, when students have more serious matters to confront, a counselor must be available. When the counseling staff works closely with the advisors to define spheres of action for each, the students will be the beneficiaries.

Students benefit from personal contact with an adult, and they see the advisory program as a place where the democratic process can occur easily.

Evaluation Procedures

Because adolescence is a time when egos are very fragile and the smallest bit of feedback, no matter how benign, can be seen as critical, educators need to be especially sensitive to assessment issues. Students are becoming more independent socially and intellectually and can, therefore, play a more active role in the assessment process. If they help to establish criteria, peer evaluate, and self-evaluate, they will be well on their way to becoming more independent in determining their own growth and achievement. Goals for middle school learning become more oriented towards using their minds to think critically and less about mastering basic skills. Assessment procedures must reflect this by balancing between product and process measures, between summative and formative evaluation. While it is important that all students experience some success in school, adolescence is especially critical because it is a time when many unsuccessful students mentally check out and eventually physically drop out.

Parent Involvement

It may come as no surprise, but parental involvement declines during middle school years. By the time students are sixteen, only fifty percent of parents report even moderate involvement at the local school (Carnegie Council on Adolescent Development, 1989). While there may be a variety of reasons why this occurs, there are schools that have been quite successful at increasing and maintaining parent involvement.

First, middle schools need to offer parents important roles in school governance. There needs to be an active process of keeping parents informed both about individual class progress and school activities. Many parents return to the work force when their children become teenagers, so schools need to design meaningful ways for parents to contribute, even if they are unable to assist during school hours. Surveying parents as to how they can help and finding ways to draw upon their strengths is most beneficial. Using parents or grandparents as guest speakers in classrooms is an excellent way to make positive connections. In addition, extracurricular activities can be supported or led by parents or interested community members. Often families need a support group. Parent-Teacher organizations can establish parenting classes or arrange for special family workshops. These activities not only help parents connect with each other and helpful professionals, but they enable families to see the school community as a welcoming place to ask for assistance in time of crisis.

Connecting with Communities

Since the early 1980s, communities have been designing programs to

Goals for middle school learning become more oriented towards using their minds to think critically and less about mastering basic skills.

help provide access to health and social services for young adolescents and their families. Since these young people are on school campuses daily, one logical place to house these support services is on or near school sites. A "full-service school" provides facilities for health clinics, mental health counseling, social service agencies, and dental health care. These programs often include youth resource centers as well as continuing education for the entire family. For example, Hanshaw Middle School in Stanislaus County, California, offers classes in computers, parenting, and high school equivalence. (Carnegie Council on Adolescent Development, 1989).

Many middle schools form partnerships with businesses. The Adopt-a-School Program is one such program where a business establishes a relationship with a neighboring school. Students visit the business in class groups or in individual mentorship programs. Employees volunteer in classrooms or as guest speakers. Usually there is some financial support from the businesses in the form of material support or scholarships.

Many middle schools form partnerships with businesses.

While it is positive and beneficial for communities to reach out to young people, students also benefit greatly when they reach out and help the community in some way. Many schools today are realizing that service learning projects connected with course curriculum or through extracurricular clubs are academically helpful, as well as helpful in building responsibility and self-esteem in young people.

Concluding Remarks

It is possible to design and implement developmentally responsive schools for middle level students. Such schools would be communities of learners in which all stakeholders—students, teachers, parents, and community members—are active participants in the intellectual, physical, emotional, social, and moral development of young adolescents. Imagine the future of young people when middle schools like the ones described here exist across this country!

Middle School Curriculum

What Is Curriculum?

The seemingly easy answer to this question is "a course of study"—
a definition that follows naturally from the Latin meaning of the
word "currere" to run a course. Curriculum theorists have found the
question and the answer to be more complex and the implications for
teachers and students to be significant. A structure offered by John
Goodlad (1979) suggests the wide range of possible ways of thinking about curriculum. He identifies five domains of curriculum:

- ◆ ideological or ideal: curriculum written by specialists
  and published in textbooks from national organizations

- ◆ formal: curriculum sanctioned by the state and/or local
  school boards

- ◆ perceived: curriculum as defined by teachers, parents,
  and community members

- ◆ operational: curriculum as it actually happens in classrooms, despite the ideal, formal, or perceived curricula
  defined above

The seemingly easy
answer to this question
is "a course of study"—
a definition that follows
naturally from the
Latin meaning of the
word "currere:" to run
a course.

◆ experiential: curriculum as the students experience it
and relate to it

It seems safe to assume that within and among these domains, the relevant players have at least somewhat differing goals. Even if there is some agreement on what is to be taught and learned, there may be differences in what the desired end is. Should the curriculum address intellectual, social, personal, or vocational goals? Should the sixth grade science class primarily aim toward intellectual development, as the state school board member urged in the curriculum framework? Or, should it aim toward the vocational skills desired by the parents? What about the social goals of the cooperative groups devised by the teacher? Or, perhaps, should it focus on the increased self-esteem and personal growth desired by the sixth graders themselves? Obviously, these goals are not mutually exclusive, and, in fact, as a nation "we want it all" when it comes to the aims of schooling (Goodlad, 1979).

Thus, the question "What is curriculum?" is more difficult to answer than might first be expected. The different domains of curriculum and the preferred goals of the participants will color how any person responds to the question.

When middle school teachers, working together or alone, make decisions about what the curriculum will be in a given year in a particular classroom, it is a good idea to keep in mind the complexity of the work. Trying to reconcile the five domains of curriculum so that there is a match of sorts among them is indeed a daunting task. Teachers do not have the luxury of distance enjoyed by textbook writers, curriculum specialists, and school board members who adopt sometimes lofty curriculum statements. Teachers live in a more interesting, messy, and exciting curriculum sphere. While some teachers ignore these features of their lives and teach to the text or to the curriculum framework, most teachers try to be more responsive to their surroundings. They deliberately adapt the ideological and formal curricula they are given in light of their students, resources, subject area expertise, and school site expectations—resulting in the perceived curriculum of the teacher.

Trying to reconcile the five domains of curriculum so that there is a match of sorts among them is indeed a daunting task.

Curriculum and Middle Level Students
Perhaps the most interesting recent development in thinking about middle school curriculum is the realization that the experiential curriculum—the curriculum lived by the students—is the place where teachers and curriculum policy makers ought to start when they make curriculum decisions. Using what we know about young adolescent development, what guesses can we make as to how middle grades

students will experience the curriculum their teachers implement? Increasingly in the 1990s, middle school curriculum developers have called for centering the curriculum around the needs, interests, problems, and concerns of young adolescents as they grow into productive and committed members of their society (Beane, 1990). Instead of viewing the subject areas as sacred monoliths to be approached with caution and great respect, middle level educators must examine these subjects with one eye firmly on the ten to fourteen-year-olds who will try to make sense of them. It is, then, an especially wise teacher who thinks of the curriculum from the students' point of view. How the experiential curriculum plays out is easily the most important of Goodlad's five domains—it is, after all, the real learning that takes place in the students that keeps all the other parties (teachers, administrators, parents, and others) engaged.

When the curriculum question is addressed in this way, traditional subject matter is not dismissed so much as it is put to the test of its relevance to young adolescence. Stevenson (1992) found that this examination leads to five caveats about appropriate curriculum selection for middle school classrooms:

When the curriculum question is addressed in this way, traditional subject matter is not dismissed so much as it is put to the test of its relevance to young adolescence.

◆ seek balance between students' needs (physical, cognitive, social, emotional, moral, and linguistic) and external requirements, such as curriculum guides and textbooks

◆ covering the curriculum is not the same as teaching and learning

◆ seek balance between exploration and mastery of material, for both have their places in middle schooling

◆ every student must have many, many successes

◆ young adolescents want and respond to intellectual rigor

When taken together, these caveats challenge middle level educators to justify their curriculum choices in light of who their students are rather than relying on traditional appeals to the importance of the content disciplines.

A Vision of Curriculum and Instruction
Fortunately, there is some tendency toward a coherent vision of a middle level curriculum responsive to young adolescents. This vision defines two divisions of the curriculum: the core curriculum and the exploratory curriculum. Inextricably tied to the curriculum are instructional practices consistent with young adolescent needs.

Core Curriculum

The core curriculum is defined as the basics of middle school subject matter: language arts, social studies, mathematics, and science. These are the school subjects that most students study every year. Too, these are the subjects that are most likely to be mandated by state and local curriculum guides. The challenge to middle school teachers is not so much to define the academic core as it is to arrange meaningful access to the most crucial parts of it so that adolescents develop a lasting understanding of the core subjects' skills and ideas.

Language Arts

Language arts curriculum content includes reading, writing, speaking, listening skills and, as some agree, viewing. For many young adolescents who are immigrants to the United States, it also includes learning all these skills in a second language. The most important recent influence on language arts curriculum and instruction is the whole language movement, which incorporates the skills curriculum into a meaningful context of real reading and writing. Nancie Atwell's (1987) reading/writing workshop approach to language arts instruction applies whole language theory to middle school curriculum and students. In this approach, reading a wide variety of literature and engaging in all forms of writing are the substance of language arts class time. Mini-lessons to address skills in meaningful ways are inserted into the reading/writing workshop on an as-needed basis. During the middle school years, students are able to appreciate a wide range of genre in literature, from picture books and comic books to historical classics. A rich curriculum in language arts would include an opportunity to read and write a variety of materials, skills instruction embedded in the reading/writing program, instruction in reading and writing across the disciplines (content area reading and writing), along with the guidance of a teacher who models not only the love of reading and writing but also engages in them.

Social Studies

Social studies curriculum in the middle school should be responsive to and build upon the interests and growing abilities of young adolescents. The Task Force on Social Studies in the Middle Grades (1991) recommended four motifs or broad categories of important social science curriculum that are appropriate for middle grades social studies. The motifs are:

◆ development of self-esteem and identity
◆ development of ethics
◆ development of group
◆ development of a global perspective

> Social studies curriculum in the middle school should be responsive to and build upon the interests and growing abilities of young adolescents.

These motifs are a good match to young adolescents' developmental needs. Middle grade students are concerned with their own development, and their interest in self can be generalized to a fascination with others—including others who have lived, or are currently living, quite different lives from theirs. As their moral reasoning becomes more sophisticated, their interest in ethical issues such as prejudice and racism grows. Their interest in living well with others is easily linked with the skills and values necessary to democratic citizenship. A strong sense of belonging to the local and global community is also appropriate in middle grades social studies. For this reason, service learning is a particularly apt teaching/learning strategy at this age (Andrus, 1995). Service learning engages students in meaningful service to their community while accomplishing important curriculum objectives. The social sciences—economics, geography, history, politics, psychology, and sociology—are the disciplines through which young adolescents can imagine their own relationship to the society in which they live. When well taught through active learning strategies, the social studies curriculum can help prepare young adolescents to make both immediate and lifelong contributions to their society.

Mathematics

Mathematics curriculum in middle schools emphasizes putting mathematics in context to give it meaning—a considerable contrast to traditional approaches to mathematics that emphasize procedural skill building and memorization of algorithms. Constructing meaning from mathematics involves discovering how mathematics can be applied to realistic problems. In such problems, there is no simple answer that calls for ready recall of simple formulae from one branch of mathematics—for example, measurement or geometry. Most realistic problems are more messy than that and may be solved through multiple rather than single paths. Instead of having teachers tell middle level students the one way to solve a problem, this approach encourages students to develop their own problem-solving strategies. Often, concrete representations (manipulatives) are appropriate learning tools, but young adolescents need to discover mathematical relationships on their own. The teacher's role in this discovery process is to fashion learning activities that motivate and support students as they grapple with the problem. On the surface, students may appear to be doing less mathematics because the traditional worksheets and list of problems at the end of the chapter are missing. These have been replaced with fewer problems which require deeper investigation to solve.

> Constructing meaning from mathematics involves discovering how mathematics can be applied to realistic problems.

Science

Science education in middle schools parallels some of the same themes as mathematics. Just as mathematics has become more discovery oriented, so has science education. Activities that emphasize divergent thinking and multiple paths to explore are the hallmark of science instruction. The content of science has not changed, but there is a greater emphasis on problem-solving and open-ended processes rather than on memorization of minute facts about the natural world—the parts of a crayfish, for example. Instead of this memorization, the adaptations the crayfish has made as it evolved are important, and the larger concept of evolution and adaptation is worthy of the students' and teacher's time. Middle school science has moved from textbook-based exercises to hands-on, minds-on instruction. Even with simple materials, young adolescents are able to learn complex concepts through experiences such as building simple musical instruments to learn concepts related to sound.

The new middle school science classroom has broken down its walls so that science knowledge is applied to real-life situations. Connections to home, businesses, museums, and science centers help to make science relevant in the middle level students' eyes. For example, studying tectonic plates and earthquakes may be uninteresting to young adolescents until an assignment asks them to conduct safety surveys of their homes. When they identify personal belongings that are likely to be lost because their homes are not earthquake prepared, the abstract becomes more meaningful.

Middle school science education has been a leader in kindergarten through twelfth grade science in the move toward an integrated science curriculum. Instead of separate courses or units on earth science, physical science, and life science, students now study scientific concepts through a thematic approach. Themes such as energy, patterns of change, and systems/interactions incorporate important content from all the science disciplines. When the curriculum is integrated in this manner, students are more likely to make connections among abstract concepts. Two concepts seemingly not related—like photosynthesis in life science and electricity in physical science— are, in fact, quite similar in that they both involve forms of energy. In the past, these were treated as isolated scientific concepts, but students are now encouraged to see their common elements.

Exploratory Curriculum

The exploratory curriculum consists of a wide range of school subjects that have long been deemed fruitful for the school experience of young adolescents. In junior high schools, these were called electives, and students chose a limited number of these subjects to com-

> When the curriculum is integrated in this manner, students are more likely to make connections among abstract concepts.

plement their required or core courses. Traditionally, music, art, physical education, foreign languages, industrial arts (for boys), and home economics (for girls) were offered as either half-year or full-year courses. Often, one or another of these were required at certain grade levels, and the remaining courses were left to student and parent choice. Typically, students would have fewer openings in their schedules than there were subjects available, so the dilemma of "If I take Spanish, then I can't take art" was the rule.

Middle schools take a different view of these curriculum areas. We know that young adolescents deal with finding themselves in terms of self-perception, skills, and interests in this phase of personality development. They need opportunities to sample many possibilities before their self-images are set in terms of "I'm a terrible artist," or "I'm clumsy," or "I don't like to cook." Forcing a young adolescent to choose one of these curriculum areas to the exclusion of another can have the effect of cutting off a potential interest in a sport, hobby, or vocation before the youngster has a chance to explore it. Even if a thirteen-year-old student does not exhibit a desire or talent for becoming a skilled artist, there is every possibility that with encouragement, he or she will grow into an adult who enjoys sketching or water colors, or one who uses an artistic sense in her career in advertising, or simply one who enjoys art in everyday life and in formal art exhibits. When schools create schedules that make it impossible for the student to dabble in art as well as Spanish, they are taking a narrow view of educating the whole student for lifelong fulfillment.

Thus, middle schools approach these curriculum areas as subjects that all students should explore to some degree—not enough to master the subjects but enough to provide a base for further learning. This stance is a considerable challenge, given the scarcity of time in any school schedule. The challenge is even greater when schools update the list of exploratory subjects. In addition to art and music, other performing arts such as drama and dance are appropriate areas of study. Industrial arts has been transformed into technology education, including sophisticated use of robots and computers, in an effort to teach students a much wider range of skills to add to those of the traditional metal and wood shops. Home economics has become family living, often becoming the repository of topics such as budgeting and nutrition. As well, both of these courses have become coed instead of single sex. Physical education often shares sex or health education responsibility with the science curriculum. Instead of one foreign language, middle schools might offer courses in languages and culture, with more than one language area explored. Computers have become a force in the middle school exploratory curriculum, with basic keyboarding and programming skills taught.

Typically, students would have fewer openings in their schedules than there were subjects available, so the dilemma of "If I take Spanish, then I can't take art" was the rule.

Middle schools incorporate all these curriculum areas and more into the exploratory area in many creative ways. One way is to organize the course topics in an exploratory wheel, where the many subjects are offered in a succession of short courses, usually six to nine weeks long, depending on the grading period used by the school. In this way, every student can experience four to six subjects each year rather than the one or two that would have been possible under the old electives framework. In this scheme, all the students in a given grade level finish the school year with identical courses, but they have taken them at different times of the year. For teachers, this arrangement means they have new students periodically and repeat the same course multiple times during the school year.

A second approach to exploratory is to arrange those subjects that are seen as most important by state or local authorities—for example, physical education or computers—in a wheel and then leave some time in the students' schedules for special interest activities. Many of these activity mini-courses are devised by teachers who have interests or abilities in a particular area so that exploratory courses are taught by core curriculum teachers as well as teachers of foreign language, art, etc. Often, these courses meet during a special time in the school week—not necessarily every day. These special activity courses incorporate the skills appropriate for young adolescent learning but in ways that appeal to their out-of-school interests. For example, activity courses in cartoons, crafts, or quilt design engage students in skills from the art curriculum, but these are packaged around specific high-interest topics. Courses that do not seem to have a base in a particular school subject area, may, nonetheless, incorporate skills from across the curriculum. These courses may address gardening, sports, science fiction, movie making, creating collections, fishing, and exploring on the Internet. The array of courses of this type is limited only by the talents, training, and interests of teachers who wish to organize them. Students should also be surveyed as to their interests. Exploratory courses are likely to change over time. This type of change is important if the curriculum is to be responsive to teachers and students.

In any exploratory program, there must be a balance between more academic courses such as computing or foreign language and activity courses like physical education or art. Further, there must be a balance between accountability for student learning and sheer enjoyment of the course despite the level of skill exhibited. For many young adolescents, the exploratory curriculum is the part of the school day that is the most interesting and enjoyable. Those who, for any reason, have difficulty in or lack excitement about the core curriculum areas may find themselves looking forward to school each

Computers have become a force in the middle school exploratory curriculum, with basic keyboarding and programming skills taught.

day in anticipation of their exploratory experiences. Exploratory is not a curriculum add-on; it is an integral part of the middle school experience.

Integrating the Curriculum

Separating the school day and school knowledge into divisions such as mathematics and art is a comfortable tradition. Human knowledge has long been divided into such subject areas for educational purposes. These divisions were once called the trivium and quadrivium; they now go by the names of the familiar disciplines that we study in schools. For many centuries it was possible for the student to master the entire curriculum, but learning even a minute fraction of human knowledge is a formidable goal today. It is estimated that the sum of human knowledge now doubles every ten years, so we will never again approach the days when one could learn to be a master of an entire discipline.

A further difficulty for teachers is to make choices between covering the curriculum or studying particular content in-depth.

Compartmentalizing the school curriculum into the disciplines is convenient, but as John Dewey noted in 1902, the disciplines fractionalize the world of the knowing. Scores of years of throwing a bulging briefcase of unrelated bits of knowledge at students has done little to ensure meaningful learning (Harter & Gehrke, 1989). As teachers who have successfully negotiated traditional schooling ourselves, we are accustomed to the chains we wear and, thus, do not realize how unnatural it is for students to have to think in these artificial categories. A further difficulty for teachers is to make choices between covering the curriculum or studying particular content in-depth. This breadth versus depth dilemma is complicated by mandated tests, grade level expectations established by schools or districts, and the teacher's own interests and knowledge.

While there are no easy answers to the fractionalizing and the breadth versus depth challenges, one attempt to address these is integrating the curriculum so that many school subjects contribute to learning important knowledge and skills. When the curriculum is integrated, the divisions among subject areas are blurred or erased through the use of a unifying theme. In this way, the school curriculum becomes more like real life where there are no artificial boundaries conforming to school subjects. It is natural for humans to look at things holistically and to seek relationships when faced with many separate objects or phenomena. When young adolescents look ahead, they will not "do" only mathematics or art or language arts in their careers and everyday lives. Teachers who work with their students to make sense of the curriculum across disciplinary lines are assisting the students to achieve a holistic picture of the universe into which they should inquire (Goodlad, 1987).

In the middle school, it is essential that the curriculum be integrated around themes or topics that will be of interest to young adolescents (Stevenson & Carr, 1993). Teachers working together must plan carefully to keep their subject matter content at a high level while emphasizing the links among the disciplines. Integrated curriculum is not watered down content; indeed, it is high level content with which the students are expected to grapple at length. It is the most important content selected by teachers who have themselves torn apart and then reconstructed their curriculum areas so that the relationships among subject areas are apparent.

Harter and Gehrke (1989) suggested that there are many approaches to integrating the curriculum. The organizing structure could be a concept, topical approach, or problem to solve. For example, a concern with dwindling natural resources and increasing consumer consumption might lead to an integrated curriculum unit on "garbology." A second organizational approach is through important concepts that encompass much of human experience. Freedom and change are examples of such concepts. Topics that readily incorporate many disciplines are a third way to organize an integrated curriculum— early humans, for example. No matter which approach is preferred, an essential element to implementing curriculum integration in middle schools is a group of teachers—members of an interdisciplinary team—who work together to create and sustain the new curriculum.

Concluding Remarks

While early adolescence is a time of tremendous growth for students, it is also a time when much learning can and should take place. A core curriculum is essential for young people to become successful adults. Intriguing questions, immediate concerns, and interesting topics will invite young adolescents into the curriculum. In addition, there needs to be time in the school day for young people to explore what else is possible to learn about, do, and be.

> While early adolescence is a time of tremendous growth for students, it is also a time when much learning can and should take place.

Interdisciplinary Teaming

Team Organization

Interdisciplinary team organization is an increasingly popular feature of restructured middle schools. The incidence of middle grade schools reporting the use of teams has increased from 33% in 1989 (Alexander & McEwin, 1989) to 57% in 1992 (Valentine, Clark, Irvin, Keefe, & Melton, 1993). Among schools that have been consciously moving toward the middle level concept for ten or more years, the incidence of interdisciplinary teaming is an astounding 87% (George & Shewey, 1994). The adoption of interdisciplinary team organization is perhaps the most dramatic development in the middle school reform movement. Ideally, an interdisciplinary team consists of teachers who share

> The adoption of interdisciplinary team organization is perhaps the most dramatic development in the middle school reform movement.

◆ the same students

◆ responsibility for planning, teaching, and evaluating curriculum and instruction for multiple courses

◆ the same schedule, including a common planning period

◆ the same area of the school building (George & Alexander, 1993)

With these basic features in place, innumerable details can be played out by the team members. Missing one or more of these four features, the path to successful interdisciplinary teaming is considerably more difficult—some would say it is impossible. Considering the challenges inherent in establishing a successful interdisciplinary team, having these structural features in place is a reasonable starting point.

Establishing and teaching a coherent, integrated curriculum is one of many goals of an interdisciplinary team. Other goals include creating

> **Establishing and teaching a coherent, integrated curriculum is one of many goals of an interdisciplinary team.**

◆ a common vision for their student

◆ a sense of community that promotes student belonging in school

◆ shared classroom procedures, expectations, and discipline measures

◆ effective communication, especially with parents

◆ appropriate evaluation and recognition of student achievement

◆ self-governance procedure

◆ rewarding professional development for the teachers themselves

When these goals are met, interdisciplinary teams of teachers and their students become more than the sum of their parts. They become a school-within-a-school—sometimes called a village. Examples of some of the roles, policies, and procedures a team can share are illustrated in the "Team Procedures Checklist" on the following page. The more common the procedures are for students among a team of teachers, the easier it is for the students to comply. A team might also develop a team philosophy with its students such as the example on page 46.

Team Procedures Checklist

Team Name _____ Colors _____ Symbol _____

Leader _____

Secretary _____

Communications Coordinator _____

Events Coordinator _____

Curriculum Coordinator _____

Parent Coordinator _____

Community Coordinator _____

Treasurer _____

Other _____

Discipline Policies _____

_____

_____

| Substitute folders prepared |
| yes   no |
| Hall/restoom passes |
| yes   no |
| Team Calendar |
| yes   no |

Consequences	Check if Used
Warning _____	
Mediators _____	
Rudeness _____	
Talking excessively _____	
Tardiness _____	
Silliness _____	
Not following directions _____	
Other _____	
Detentions _____	
Lunch _____	
After School _____	
Time-Out Stations _____	
Loss of Privileges _____	
Outside_____	
Activity _____	
Other _____	
Team Conference _____	
Clean-up Duty _____	
Parent Conference _____	
Home Contract _____	
Referral _____	
Other _____	

Academic Guidelines
(circle or complete)

Grading standards: **Different   Uniform**

Amount of homework:

Daily   **Yes   No   Sometimes**

On weekends   **Yes   No   Sometimes**

Late work penalty:

Daily work   _____ a day

Major projects   _____ a day

If completed same day _____

Extra credit bonus:

Assignments available **Yes   No**

Bonus points _____

For typed work   **Yes   No**

Special:_____

_____

_____

Reprinted from TCM 548 How to Manage Your Middle School Classroom, *Teacher Created Materials, 1996*

Teaming

Creating a Mission Statement

Each team should always make a statement of goals and beliefs. Hang this in every classroom so you and the students get to see it often. Mission statements are sometimes seen as corny and superficial, but if you do not have a greater purpose in mind, you will not be satisfied as a team. Following is an example:

Star Team Mission Statement

Clay, Hamad, Agrippa, Rockler, Hernandez, and Orangetree

The Star Team pledges to . . .

1. Promote the academic and emotional growth of Star Team students.
2. Provide quality, challenging education.
3. Handle discipline problems firmly and consistently.
4. Strengthen learning by curriculum lining and interdisciplinary units.
5. Honor excellence with frequent assemblies and activities.
6. Recognize success with thematic celebrations.
7. Involve parents in the learning process.
8. Reach out to the community as much as possible.
9. Provide all Star students with support and encouragement.

Everyone is a star on the Star Team.

...THE STARS...

Reprinted from TCM 548 How to Manage Your Middle School Classroom, *Teacher Created Materials, 1996*

Interdisciplinary teaming is linked with many positive outcomes for both teachers and students (Arhar & Irvin, 1995). For teachers, feelings of efficacy and professional satisfaction increase when teaming is in place. Teachers report that they become more flexible and realistic in their thinking, more confident in their decision-making abilities, and more positive in self-image. They feel less isolated and less stressed when they team. Negative results for teachers are mostly associated with the early stages of teaming, when frustration grows due to the complexity of the tasks facing the team.

These teacher effects have their own impact on students. Increased teacher efficacy and satisfaction are strongly associated with increased student achievement (Arhar & Irvin, 1995). So, although we do not have direct evidence linking teacher teaming with student achievement, a relationship between them exists. In addition, students in interdisciplinary teams have fewer discipline problems, greater feelings of engagement in school, and better student-teacher relationships.

As one might imagine, the success of an interdisciplinary team is due to no small effort. Communication among teammates is an extremely important ingredient. This is most easily facilitated by the scheduling of a common planning period.

Support from administration is essential. Principals need to know that teaming can be invigorating and, occasionally, draining. Members of the team must have time to do some long-range planning, as well as attend workshops and inservice training in areas that enhance the teaming process. While support is important, team members must also be empowered and given autonomy to make many of the day-in-and-day-out decisions.

> Finally, teachers on a team must come to realize that they are not responsible for only one subject area anymore.

Finally, teachers on a team must come to realize that they are not responsible for only one subject area anymore. They teach the whole child. In reality, team success is measured in teacher commitment of time and energy. No team can succeed without it.

Interdisciplinary Curriculum Units

Often the desire to team exists in middle school faculties, but the task simply looks too overwhelming. A sound recommendation is to start small—that is, do not attempt to mesh all the curriculum of all the relevant teachers all year long. In the beginning stages of an interdisciplinary team, the design and implementation of one interdisciplinary unit of instruction in the year is cause for considerable celebration. It takes time for team members to come to know each other and the curriculum areas they are planning to integrate. A long-term commitment of resources, energy, and good humor may well increase the staying power of a team.

Teams create integrated curriculum units in much the same way that individual teachers create interdisciplinary or thematic units. An excellent source is *Integrated Thematic Units* (Seely, or thematic 1995). The difference between team and individual planning lies in the early stages, when the myriad pieces of each teacher's curriculum area are placed on the table, as it were, and the search for some sense—some connection— begins. The first step is to identify a theme that lends itself to the greatest participation by all the subject areas while addressing important needs of young adolescents and the interests of the teachers. As an example, a sixth grade team might choose survival for its first interdisciplinary unit. This topic is relevant to the students, who are beginning to take steps into a world wider and more likely challenging than that of their home and neighborhood. This topic is also attractive to the teachers, whose designated curricula might include wild animals, celestial navigation, fitness, cartography, graphing, and journal writing—all of which can be worked into this theme quite easily. Once a topic is selected, the team generates ideas for activities, resources, and materials by way of a planning web. With the theme in the center of the web, ideas from all curriculum areas are contributed to the plan. An alternative method of team planning is to have team members write out the content topics, skills, and assessments that each wants to accomplish in the theme. Student input is important at this point. Team members should solicit ideas from the students about what they are most interested in learning about so ample opportunities to satisfy these needs can be incorporated. Sample planning webs and charts are on the following pages.

When this phase of planning is complete, the team members turn their attention to creating a calendar that provides variety, choice, individual and group work, and multiple sources of information. A culminating event or project will provide a suitable outlet for students to demonstrate what they have learned. For example, for the survival theme, a camp-out (in the school gym, if necessary) can include a backdrop for a display of student work, a guest speaker, and performances that summarize student learning. Page 51 highlights more ideas for a camp-out. The key is that multiple forms of assessment that cut across content areas should be incorporated into the unit, both during the unit and in the culminating project or performance.

> Teams create integrated curriculum units in much the same way that individual teachers create interdisciplinary units.

Planning Web

Use this form as a planning overview for thematic activities and assessments.

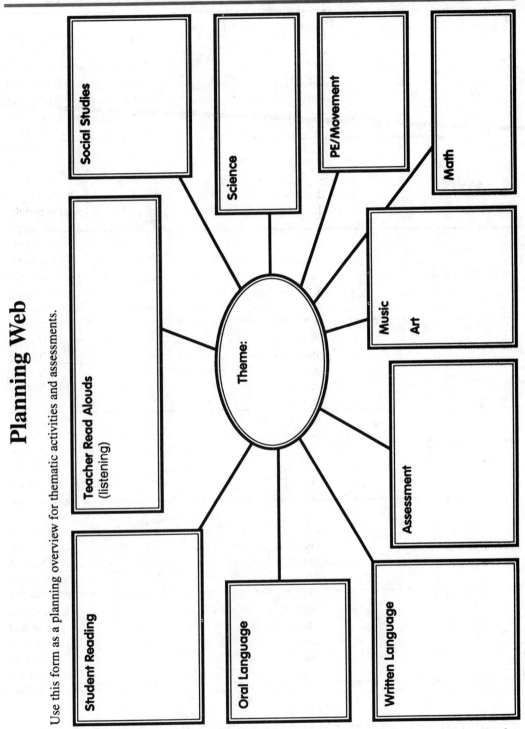

Reprinted from Workshop Notebook: Portfolios and Other Alternative Assessments, *Teacher Created Materials, 1993*

Planning Chart Form

Theme _____ Grade Level _____

	Area	Content	Skill	Assessment
Language Arts				
Social Studies				
Math				
Science				
Art/Music				
Other				

Reprinted from Workshop Notebook: Portfolios and Other Alternative Assessments, *Teacher Created Materials, 1993*

Survival Theme Night or Camp Out

Camp Out

An ideal way to culminate your extended unit on survival would be to take your class on a camping trip to practice the survival skills they have learned in a real wilderness setting. If a camping trip is not a possibility, you may want to consider having a survival theme night at your school.

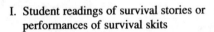

Survival Theme Night

A theme night can be an enjoyable way to close a unit. It is an especially good way to show off the students' hard work to their parents. Following is a suggested outline for how you might want to organize your theme night.

I. Student readings of survival stories or performances of survival skits

Select stories or plays that your students have written during the unit to be read or performed for the parents.

II. Student projects and reports on display for viewing

Set tables around the room with students' topographic maps, knots, survival kits, shelters, floating compass, notch calendar, animal tracks, and survival reports. Stories and flat maps can be displayed on classroom bulletin boards.

III. A ranger or other related specialist as a speaker

Ask your students if any of their parents, aunts, uncles, or grandparents have worked as park rangers, search and rescue officials, fire persons, or any other survival-related occupations. (Grandparents are often wonderful resources to tap.) If not, call your local park and recreation department or chamber of commerce for resource suggestions.

IV. Refreshments

Refreshments can be served by students.

Reprinted from TCM 604 Interdisciplinary Unit: Survival, *Teacher Created Materials, 1995*

When an interdisciplinary unit comes to a close, team members need to take time to debrief and evaluate both the curriculum and the team's performance. Especially when a team implements a new unit, chances are there will be rough spots, miscommunications, and some ideas that flop. It is helpful to remember that creating interdisciplinary units in teams of discipline-oriented teachers is a major undertaking, and that with practice, teaming becomes more fluid and more rewarding.

Concluding Remarks

Interdisciplinary Teaming is probably the most important commitment a school can make to the middle school concept. It can create a ripple effect. Teachers who share a common vision, one set of policies regarding discipline and expectations, the same students, and common planning time can go far to institute the elements of middle schools. Common planning time allows teachers to develop integrated thematic units. Integrated curriculum enables students to see curriculum as a whole and learning more relevant to their lives. The benefits of interdisciplinary teaming for schools, teachers, and students cannot be underestimated.

Instructional Practices

Responsive Practice for Young Adolescents

After examining the growth and development of the ten to fourteen-year-old, there remains little doubt that in order to be responsive to the physical, cognitive, social, and emotional demands of the age, instructional practices must be varied. Teaching strategies and techniques must also reflect the needs of the subjects studied as part of the middle school curriculum. Over the past few years, there has been a lot of information about the different ways students learn best. Certainly a middle school teacher must also respond to the learning styles of the students and provide multiple ways in which they can demonstrate their knowledge and skills. The more teaching and learning strategies the teacher has in his or her repertoire, the more successful the students will be.

One of the major goals of education in the middle grades is for students to become independent learners. We hope this goal is transparent in the list of exemplary practices that follow.

Cooperative Learning

Due to their social and emotional needs for peer interaction, middle school students do well with group activities where every member of

> Teaching strategies and techniques must also reflect the needs of the subjects studied as part of the middle school curriculum.

the group has a responsibility to learn something or complete a task. Practically all subject areas contain curricular aspects that would be well served by using a cooperative learning strategy. Cooperative learning provides a vehicle for students to take responsibility for their own learning. An important side benefit is that it is an excellent tool in dealing with students of varying levels of ability. Like all approaches, "it should not be employed 100 percent of the time. Research indicates that 60 percent is optimal" (Messick & Reynolds, 1992, p. 192).

Simulations or Role Play

Using simulations or role play, students get a chance to actually try out roles and make decisions based on those roles. These strategies appeal to the social nature of middle school students, and they are effective because of the active learning that is inherent in these techniques. Role play also allows them to experience life from another person's point of view, a very important perspective to be developed during the middle grades.

> Using simulations or role play, students get a chance to actually try out roles and make decisions based on those roles.

Individual Study Topics

Allowing students to choose a topic to research either within an established curriculum or within the wide range of human knowledge is, perhaps, the most pedagogically responsive activity possible in a middle school setting. Through this activity, students become more involved in their learning; they also are given an opportunity to deal with the burning questions that so characterize this age. Despite the open-endedness of this activity, students still need structure and plenty of time to process what they are learning. Frequent teacher-student and student-student conferences are essential.

Inquiry

In teaching for inquiry, the teacher poses a problem or question for students to resolve. Sometimes there is a correct answer; other times there are several or none. The one prerequisite is that the question should be inherently compelling. For example, Why is it easier to float in salt water? or Why did the Titanic sink? Students may conduct their inquiry in a whole group setting, in small groups, or individually. A nonjudgmental environment is essential; all thoughtful answers are valued. Successful inquiry lessons are possible in all subject areas. This approach is stimulating for middle school students who are able to think about their own thinking and who ponder questions about why things work the way they do.

Specially Designed Academic Instruction in English

Teaching strategies that are effective with English learners must take into account the underlying realities of second language learning.

On average, it takes language minority students two to three years to understand and speak a second language well enough to operate in such day-to-day situations as social conversations and basic interactions in their new schools and communities. It is understandable— but incorrect—that we assume that such students are also able to understand, read, write, and speak the academic language of their new surroundings. To become proficient at this decontextualized, cognitively demanding language takes from five to seven years of practice. English learners who may chat with and write notes to their young adolescent friends in English may not be so able to read, speak, and write in English when the topic of interest is the Articles of Confederation or division of fractions. Content area teachers need to use special teaching strategies to reach these students so that they do not fall behind or receive a watered-down curriculum compared to their native English-speaking peers. The goal of this strategy is to provide grade level content instruction in English to non-native speakers who have intermediate fluency in English. Sometimes called "sheltered instruction," but more formally known as Specially Designed Academic Instruction in English or SDAIE (suh-die), the strategy is a collection of good instructional practices: moving from familiar to unfamiliar content, moving from concrete to abstract content, moving from the whole to the part of a concept, displaying relevant visual aids around the classroom, creating a comfortable atmosphere in the classroom, increasing wait time, employing cooperative groups, assessing while teaching, attending to vocabulary development, and emphasizing depth rather than the amount of material covered in one lesson. By using SDAIE strategies, a monolingual teacher can be effective in teaching English learners while not compromising the core curriculum that all students deserve to learn (California State Department of Education, 1991).

Values Clarification

Not unlike an inquiry lesson, a values clarification lesson usually presents a problem or question about a moral dilemma or issue. Middle level students are beginning to see things from other perspectives, and they benefit greatly when moral choices and accompanying rationales are discussed in peer groups. For example, a moral dilemma such as spotting another student cheating on a test, can be discussed in class. It could involve discussing topical issues in science or social studies from different points of view. A study of slavery in the South might involve students in a discussion of the various viewpoints or even a mock trial.

Service Learning

Although community service has been accepted as an appropriate activity for young adolescents for many years, the notion that service

Not unlike an inquiry lesson, a values clarification lesson usually presents a problem or question about a moral dilemma or issue.

can be a tool for learning important curriculum content is a more recent development in middle level instructional practice. Hands-on learning of the type that takes place in the community can be a powerful experience for the students. While they learn to make a difference in their school or neighborhoods, they also learn about the school content under study. For example, a unit on environmental studies is strengthened by the students' service in conducting a cleanup at a local wilderness area. In high service/high curriculum integration situations such as this, both the community and the curriculum are well served.

Direct Instruction

Direct instruction has a place in responsive middle school classrooms. Directly imparting knowledge and demonstrating skills is important. In doing so, the teacher needs to keep in mind the needs of the middle school student. Few students, including adult students, can listen intently to a lecture for thirty or forty minutes. Direct-instruction specialists recommend that the teacher use visuals, costumes, and hands-on activities whenever possible. The teacher should find appropriate ways to have students up and out of their seats. Frequent checks for understanding, partner talks, and quick writes can break up a long direct-instruction session.

Involving students in high level discussions and asking open-ended and critical questions are hallmarks of a pedagogically responsive teacher. Students in the middle grades want to think about and actively examine all aspects of their world. Instructional practices that promote this type of investigation will lead students to become self-directed learners.

Concluding Remarks

Effective instruction in middle schools requires an extensive repertoire of teaching strategies. Balancing the demands of the formal curriculum with the developmental needs of these young adolescents is no small undertaking. Middle level teachers "must do everything possible to enhance the probability of every student being successful" (Stevenson, 1992, p. 122). The chances of reaching every student in diverse middle school classrooms increase with the variety of approaches the teacher employs. Building this repertoire of strategies is a career-long undertaking—one that keeps middle school teachers at the forefront of excellent teaching practice.

Assessment

Developing a Philosophy of Assessment

The beginning of any good teaching is to reflect upon and articulate one's beliefs about teaching and learning. Not only is this good for teaching, but it is on these beliefs that assessment practices should be based rather than the other way around. Currently, with the accountability movement in full swing, assessment often seems to drive learning. Educators are more likely to teach to the test. However, learning does not occur in linear, sequential ways, and teachers cannot always determine goals or outcomes. Teachers often alter their course in the midst of an activity, or a line of questioning may change as an insight is gained into students' strategies or understandings. What we know about the nature of teaching and learning has changed. When we believed that we could define what it is students needed to know and that it was possible to transmit this information in twelve years of schooling, then assessment tested static knowledge. The shift from knowledge transmission to inquiry and the view of students as constructors of their own knowledge has impacted not only teaching and learning but assessment as well. In short, assessment must follow the nature of learning rather than lead it. The same conditions that exist for learning must also exist for assessment.

The beginning of any good teaching is to reflect upon and articulate one's beliefs about teaching and learning.

For example, if we believe that learning is and should be social, then assessment must be collaborative and represent multiple points of view. If learning is idiosyncratic, then assessment must be adaptive, flexible, and varied. If learning is multidimensional, then so must assessment be. In its report to Congress, the Office of Technology Assessment (OTA) noted:

> *Recent research suggests that complex thinking and learning involves processes that cannot be reduced to routine, that knowledge is a complex network of information and abilities rather than a series of isolated facts and skills. According to this research, students need to be able to successfully engage in tasks that have multiple solutions and require interpretive and nuanced judgments* (Office of Technology Assessment, 1992, p. 13).

Assessment must keep pace with what we currently know about learning and teaching. Therefore, it is vital that every educator determine his or her philosophy of learning, teaching, and assessment before beginning to assess students. At the middle level, it would be especially valuable for a team to determine their philosophy together. It is valuable for students also when a teaching team has a consistent vision of assessment, as well as common late homework policies and the like. Students also benefit when a team communicates and coordinates test and project due dates so that students are not overwhelmed.

There are several professional resources available to assist in the process of developing an assessment philosophy. One highly recommended publication is a joint publication of the International Reading Association and the National Council of Teachers of English (1994). While the goals are focused on assessing literacy, they apply to all the disciplines. The authors recommend the following eleven goals with a discussion of each.

- ◆ The interests of the students are paramount in assessment.
- ◆ The primary purpose of assessment is to improve teaching and learning.
- ◆ Assessment must reflect and allow for critical inquiry into curriculum and instruction.
- ◆ Assessments must recognize and reflect the intellectually and socially complex nature of reading and writing and the important roles of school, home, and society in literacy development.

Assessment must keep pace with what we currently know about learning and teaching.

- Assessment must be fair and equitable.
- The consequences of an assessment procedure are the first and most important consideration in establishing the validity of the assessment.
- The teacher is the most important agent of assessment.
- The assessment process should involve multiple perspectives and sources of data.
- Assessment must be based in the school community.
- All members of the educational community— students, parents, teachers, administrators, policy makers, and the public—must have a voice in the development, interpretation, and reporting of assessment.
- Parents must be involved as active, essential participants in the assessment process.

Note, too, how closely some of these recommendations follow those made for the curriculum for young adolescents. Similarly, the National Council of Teachers of Mathematics and the Mathematical Sciences Educational Board (1995) have developed standards for assessment. These can be summarized as the following:

- Assess what is important.
- Assessment should enhance student learning.
- Assessment should promote equity.
- Assessment should enhance instruction.

Reform in Mathematics Assessment provides a full discussion of these (Bennett, 1994).

One means of assessment which effectively encompasses many of these principles is observation or "kidwatching." The following page is a form which will assist a teacher in doing just that.

> **One means of assessment which effectively encompasses many of these principles is observation or "kidwatching."**

"Kid-Watcher" Form

If you talked about "kid-watching" at Back-to-School Night, you can have this form ready to hand to visiting parents when they come to your room. (It can also be given to visiting administrators and teachers.)

"Kid-Watcher" Form

"Kid-watching," or observing students in the act of learning, is an official part of portfolio assessment. Please observe the activities going on in the room and make notes on this form. You may concentrate on your own child or on the whole group. Please place this form on the teacher's desk before you leave. It will become part of our records. Thank you.

Learning activity I observed (language arts, math, etc.):

_____

Name of student or type of group (large, small, cooperative, partners, etc.):

_____

Please describe what the students were doing (reading a book, writing an essay or story, having a discussion, etc.).

_____

_____

What was most interesting to you about this observation?

_____

_____

_____

_____   _____
Kid-Watcher   *Date of Observation*

Reprinted from TCM 506 Middle School Assessment, *Teacher Created Materials, 1994*

Responsive Assessment

When developing a philosophy of assessment, it is vital to keep in mind the characteristics of young adolescents and effective instruction for them. We know that growth in one area of development does not mean growth in another. Many adolescents who look fully developed physically or socially may not have developed emotionally or intellectually. As described in chapter one, a young adolescent is never fully in one stage of development. Because a student is successful in one domain does not mean he or she is successful in others. Therefore, it is vital that we use multiple measures and get a full picture of what each student is capable of doing. Team teaching and common planning time facilitate this. As most teachers know, the same student can appear very different in science class, music, and physical education. Encouraging students to represent their knowledge in various ways at various points of time, and on a variety of tasks, provides the best opportunity for success. It also provides information to the teacher on how best to teach that student.

Because students are developing at so many different rates, assessment that addresses individual achievement rather than comparison to peers is more appropriate. During this time, even the most popular student is comparing him or herself to others and falling short in some way. Assessment which demonstrates individual growth over time is critical during middle school.

Most young adolescents have mastered basic concepts (reading, writing, multiplying, dividing, reading maps, etc.) and are learning to use their minds, not just attain knowledge. Assessment must measure not only the knowledge they have gained but also how they apply and use it. Because young adolescents are fluctuating between concrete operations and formal operations, both concrete and abstract concepts should be part of an assessment plan. At the same time, as young adolescents become more reflective and aware of their own thinking processes, they should be given many opportunities to communicate their ideas through journals and learning logs. Students and teachers benefit from students making explicit their thoughts about their reading, writing, mathematical, or scientific process. Reflection through writing or discussion also gives students an opportunity to explore those gray areas in which they are discovering what they think, feel, and believe.

Because identity formation is predominant in young adolescents' lives, opportunities to explore who they are in a safe environment is important to them. Good teaching and assessment provide this safe place in which students experiment with who they are and what they know without fear of being criticized unduly. Effective middle

Assessment which demonstrates individual growth over time is critical during middle school.

school teachers are particularly sensitive to students' work as an extension of who they are, and they respond accordingly. It is easy for middle school students to perceive themselves as failures and begin to lose interest in school. As Stevenson (1992) pointed out, students must have many, many successes. Therefore, assessment that provides valuable feedback and also points to individual success is vital.

Data Sources

Information about students from multiple sources, such as other teachers, peers, parents, self, and community members will provide the most complete picture of the students' ability and growth. It is impossible in this chapter to fully describe assessment practices. However, there are many good resources currently available for teachers. We hope you will find the following information helpful and enjoy the lengthy list of additional resources in the reference section.

Teacher-Made Tests

Research shows that middle school teachers use teacher-made tests and use them more often than elementary teachers (Airasian, 1989). Despite the drive to challenge students to engage in higher level thinking, middle school teachers, more than elementary or high school teachers, rely almost exclusively on questions at the literal comprehension or knowledge level. As discussed previously, assessment needs to measure more than knowledge. Tests which require problem solving, critical thinking, and application of content knowledge are more valuable to teachers and students. Students can even help write questions for tests while learning about Bloom, Engelhard, Furst, Hill, and Krathwohl's (1956) taxonomy. More credit can be given for questions which require more thought, such as those at the application or analysis level of the taxonomy, rather than just comprehension.

Observation/Anecdotal Records

While observation has been found to be a powerful assessment technique, teachers receive little training in using it effectively. It may be the most prevalent assessment tool used by classroom teachers. Elementary teachers rely on it more than high school teachers, and language arts teachers more than mathematics and science teachers (Stiggins & Bridgeford, 1985). The best kind of observational instruments involve directly watching and systematically recording behavior—for example, counting how many times John speaks in a small group discussion. Carrying around a seating chart while leading a class discussion and recording who participates can provide a contrast to the small group record and give valuable information about participation in large and small groups or whether a student is more successful at verbal response than at written. Observation can be recorded after the fact, but memory tends to be less reliable and judgment can creep in, which makes observation information less reliable. Anecdotal records are one way to avoid inaccurate accounts. These are simply dated, running lists of comments made by the teacher about a student. Sometimes anecdotal records appear in portfolios because they are an excellent way to document growth over time. The following two pages are examples of ways to keep anecdotal records.

Anecdotal Records/Classroom List—Example

This is an example of how to keep a running classroom list of observed behaviors. The comments are written with the idea of being transferred to individual forms, and may be elaborated upon at the end of the day.

- -

Record of Observed Behavior

DATE	STUDENT'S NAME	COMMENT

Reprinted from TCM 506 Middle School Assessment, *Teacher Created Materials, 1994*

A Simple Method for Checking Almost Anything

Checklists do not have to be complicated. This is a simple method of checking almost anything, from the most difficult concepts to the people who are or are not taking part in class discussions.

You will need a large paper divided into squares or rectangles. A large desk-pad-type calendar is perfect for this. Use this like a seating chart, writing in the names of the students in their approximate seat locations. You can have one for each of your classes and keep them stacked on your desk. Be sure to label them clearly (PERIOD 2—MATH) so you don't grab the wrong one by mistake.

Make a simple key. If you are observing a class discussion, you can use a + for a correct response, a - for a response that reflects a need for individual instruction, a ? for a student's question, and so on.

You can see in the filled-out chart below that Marty asked a question, Tam needs some help, and Robert dominated the discussion by giving eight correct responses.

Check Chart for _Class Discussion_

Marty ?	Ben ✔ –	Maria +	Gabe ?	Tam – – –	Vince + +	Danny
Julie ?	Mary +	Fran + + +	Robert + + ? + + + + + +	Jenny + –	Marilyn ??	Carl
Pam + +	Luan + +	Betsy – ?				
				David + +	Tuan + + +	Liz – + ?
				Roger + +	Mario – + +	Terri ???

Key

? = student has a question   ✔ = participation

+ = correct response   – = needs individual attention

Reprinted from TCM 506 Middle School Assessment, *Teacher Created Materials, 1994*

Interviews, Questionnaires, and Conferences

Another means to obtaining information about students' attitudes, interests, and opinions is to ask them. Interviews, questionnaires, and conferences can be easily adapted to particular groups or individuals. Interviews and conferences can be structured or unstructured, provide immediate feedback, and give the teacher and student valuable one-on-one time. When students feel comfortable and free to talk, interviews and conferences, while time consuming, can be the most valuable time spent in assessment.

Authentic Assessment

Almost every state is investigating or has implemented alternative assessment strategies which aim to measure how well students apply knowledge. This trend is due to dissatisfaction with norm-referenced, multiple-choice tests and the inadequate information they give us. Norm-referenced tests tell more about how students compare to each other and little about how much students have learned. Authentic assessment (sometimes referred to as alternative assessment) provides a better picture about what is being learned in the classroom. It is assessment based on authentic performance based tasks. It is a more balanced picture because it looks at a students' work over time. For an in-depth discussion of alternative assessments, see *Authentic Assessment* (Ryan, 1994).

Portfolios

While portfolios have been a standard form of assessment in other professions, they are currently gaining popularity and credibility in classrooms. A few states—Vermont, Michigan, and Kentucky—have even adopted portfolios statewide. Portfolios can best be summarized as "collect, select, reflect." Students collect schoolwork, awards, artwork, documentation of hobbies, interests, etc., over a specified period of time. Then, they select the pieces that best represent themselves and their growth. Finally, the students reflect (through writing) upon what they have learned and achieved as represented by the pieces they have selected. A sample reflection form can be found on page 68.

Portfolios are very flexible and can be adapted to meet whatever goal the teacher has in mind. A portfolio can be a showcase portfolio in which the student puts forth only those pieces of work which reflect his best. A collection portfolio contents form is located on page 69. Or, a portfolio can be a growth portfolio in which a student puts in pieces which are not the best samples but which, over time, show how the work has improved. A portfolio can also be a place where students demonstrate talents and abilities they have outside of school, and not usually seen in school, like Eagle Scout badges, 4-H ribbons, dance recital pictures, drama programs, or evidence of other artistic talents or even volunteer work.

Portfolio assessment is particularly appropriate for young adolescents, especially when utilized in a team or village setting. First, portfolios provide a vehicle for collecting information about growth and improvement over time. Second, the teachers on the team (and the students themselves) can get a full picture of a student's growth and ability across disciplines. Third, portfolios ask students to reflect on their own knowledge and progress and assess themselves.

The Reflective Essay—
Student Prompt

Look through the writing samples in your portfolios and put them in order by date.

Take time to reflect upon the changes you see over a period of time. Consider such things as fluency, clarity, organization, mechanics, and spelling.

What do you do now that you did not do before? What do you do better? What improvements would you still like to make?

Write an essay reflecting on your own progress.

_____

_____

_____

_____

_____

_____

_____

_____

_____

_____

_____

_____

_____

What's in it?—Collection Portfolio

Attach a copy of this form, or a variation of it, to the inside front cover of each Collection Portfolio so interested people will know what they are looking at. Save yourself hours of individual explanations by having students check categories and list pieces of work as they place them in the portfolios.

- -

This Collection Portfolio is the property of

_____

It contains samples of my work in these subject areas:

☐ Writing
_____
_____
_____

☐ Math
_____
_____

☐ Social Studies
_____
_____
_____

☐ Science
_____
_____
_____

☐ Art/Music
_____
_____
_____

Reprinted from TCM 506 Middle School Assessment, *Teacher Created Materials, 1994*

What Does this Mean for Teachers and Students?

The most effective assessment is that which is driven by a philosophy. Teachers (or teams of teachers) should sit down and determine their beliefs about teaching and learning and how they can be assessed. The clearer we are in our goals, the clearer we can be to our students. At some point, students need to be invited into the assessment process. Students, and especially young adolescents, appreciate being involved in the process of teaching and assessing. Students can join in at the beginning, middle, end, or at all three times. A truly democratic classroom has students help to determine assessment goals and criteria for assignments. Students can also provide feedback during group work, for a piece of writing, a scientific experiment, or a math problem. The more independent they become in assessing each other and themselves, the more capable they become in determining how they are growing, learning, and achieving their goals.

> Students, and especially young adolescents, appreciate being involved in the process of teaching and assessing.

The other partner who needs to be a part of the assessment process is parents. The clearer parents are about a teacher's goals, the more supportive they can be of the teacher and the more able they are to assist the student. A parent can also provide valuable insight about his or her child. When teachers ask for parents to reflect, respond, and contribute to the assessment process, they acknowledge that education is a shared responsibility between home and school.

Concluding Remarks

Alternative ways of looking at assessment that are responsive to the characteristics of young adolescents are in keeping with the recommendations of *Turning Points* (Carnegie Council on Adolescent Development, 1989), *This We Believe* (National Middle School Association, 1995), and other middle level reform documents. Their vision of exemplary middle level practices brings to mind a classroom in which students are actively engaged in their own learning. The parents of the student are invited in to provide their own insight. Community members may even visit the classroom for a portfolio day in which they give students feedback on their portfolios. The teacher is helping the students determine and clarify the assessment task and its criteria, participating in the ongoing assessment of work in progress, and proposing alternative ways that students might meet the proposed goals. Everyone who has a stake in a student's learning has a voice.

Selected Resources for Middle Level Education

Reform Reports (Government and Private Foundations)

Carnegie Council on Adolescent Development. (1989). <u>Turning points: Preparing American youth for the 21st century</u>. New York: Carnegie Corporation of New York.

Carnegie Council on Adolescent Development. (1995). <u>Great transitions: Preparing adolescents for a new century</u>. New York: Carnegie Corporation of New York.

Council of Chief State School Officers. (1992). <u>Principles to support: Higher order learning in the middle grades</u>. Washington, DC: Author.

Council of Chief State School Officers. (1992). <u>Turning points: States in action: An interim report of The Middle Grade School State Policy Initiative</u>. Washington, DC: Author.

Filby, N. N., Lee, G. V., & Lambert, V. (1990). <u>Middle grades reform: A casebook for school leaders</u>. San Francisco, CA: Far West Regional Laboratory.

Lewis, A. C. (1990). <u>Making it in the middle : The why and how of excellent schools for young urban adolescents</u>. New York: The Edna McConnell Clark Foundation.

Lewis, A. C. (1991). <u>Gaining ground: The highs and lows of urban middle school reform, 1989–91</u>. New York: The Edna McConnell Clark Foundation.

Lewis, A. C. (1993). <u>Changing the odds: Middle school reform in progress, 1991–93</u>. New York: The Edna McConnell Clark Foundation.

Middle Grades Task Force. (1987). <u>Caught in the middle: Educational reform for young adolescents in California public schools</u>. Sacramento: California State Department of Education.

Middle Level Teachers and Teacher Education

Alexander, W., & McEwin, C. K. (1988). <u>Preparing to teach at the middle level</u>. Columbus, OH: National Middle School Association.

Butler, D. A., Davies, M. A., & Dickinson, T. S. (1991). <u>On site: Preparing middle level teachers through field experiences</u>. Columbus, OH: National Middle School Association.

McEwin, C. K., & Dickinson, T. S. (1995). <u>The professional development of middle level teachers: Profiles of successful programs</u>. Columbus, OH: National Middle School Association.

McEwin, C. K., Dickinson, T. S., Erb, T. O., & Scales, P. C. (1995). <u>A vision of excellence: Organizing principles for middle grades teacher preparation</u>. Columbus, OH: National Middle School Association.

National Association of State Directors of Teacher Education and Certification. (1994). <u>Outcome-based teacher education standards for the elementary, middle, and high school levels</u>. Dubuque, IA: Kendall/Hunt.

National Board for Professional Teaching Standards. (1992). <u>Early adolescence/generalist standards for national board certification</u>. Washington, DC: Author.

National Board for Professional Teaching Standards. (1993). <u>Early adolescence/English language arts standards for national board certification</u>. Washington, DC: Author.

National Middle School Association. (1991). <u>National Middle School Association/National Council for Accreditation of Teacher Education-approved curriculum guidelines</u>. Columbus,

National Middle School Association. (1991). National Middle School Association/National Council for Accreditation of Teacher Education-approved curriculum guidelines. Columbus, OH: Author.

National Middle School Association. (1991). Professional certification and preparation for the middle level. Columbus, OH: Author.

Scales, P. C. (1992). Windows of opportunity: Improving middle grades teacher preparation. Chapel Hill, NC: Center for Early Adolescence.

Scales, P. C., & McEwin, C. K. (1994). Growing pains: The making of America's middle school teachers. Chapel Hill, NC: Center for Early Adolescence.

Stowell, L. A., Rios, F. A., McDaniel, J. E., & Kelly, M. G. (1993). Casting wide the net: Portfolios in teacher education. Middle School Journal, 25(2), 61–67.

Swaim, J., & Stefanich, G. (in press). Meeting the standards: Improving middle level education. Columbus, OH: National Middle School Association.

Resources for Teachers

California Department of Education. (1993). Caught in the middle (videotape series). Sacramento: Author.

California League of Middle Schools. (1988–1993). Practitioner's Monographs #1–15. Irvine, CA: Author.

George, P., & Alexander, W. (1992). The exemplary middle school. Orlando, FL: Harcourt Brace Jovanovich College Publishers.

Hill, B. C., & Ruptic, B. (1994). Practical aspects of authentic assessment: Putting the pieces together. Norwood, MA: Christopher-Gordon.

Mitman, A. L., & Lambert, V. (1992). Instructional challenge: A casebook for middle grade educators. San Francisco, CA: Far West Regional Laboratory.

National Middle School Association. (1995). This we believe. Columbus, OH: Author.

Rhodes, L. K., & Shanklin, N. (1993). Windows into literacy: Assessing learners K–8. Portsmouth, NH: Heinemann.

Stevenson, C. (1992). Teaching ten to fourteen-year-olds. New York: Longman.

Journals

Current Issues in Middle Level Education (West Georgia College)
Middle School Journal (NMSA)
Research in Middle Level Education (NMSA)

Professional Organizations

National Middle School Association
2600 Corporate Exchange Dr., Suite 370
Columbus, OH 43231
800-528-NMSAWorld Wide Web site: http://snow-white.gac.peachnet.edu/talk/org/edu/nmsa

Center for the Education of Young Adolescents
128 Doudna Hall
University of Wisconsin at Platteville
Platteville, WI 53818-3099
608-342-1276

References

Airasian, P. W. (1989). Classroom assessment and educational improvement. In L. W. Anderson (Ed.), The effective teacher (pp. 333–342). New York: Random House.

Alexander, W. M., & McEwin, C. K. (1989). Schools in the middle: Status and progress. Columbus, OH: National Middle School Association.

Andrus, E. (1995). Service learning and middle school students: The perfect fit. In Y. Siu-Runyan & C.V. Faircloth (Eds.), Beyond separate subjects: Integrative learning at the middle level (pp.167–186). Norwood, MA: Christopher-Gordon.

Arhar, J., & Irvin, J. (1995). Middle school journal. Columbus, OH: National Middle School Association.

Atwell, N. (1987). In the middle. Portsmouth, NH: Heinemann.

Beane, J. (1990). Rethinking the middle school curriculum. Middle School Journal, 21(5), 1–5.

Bennett, T. R. (1994). Reform in mathematics assessment: The concerns new assessment practices are trying to address. (Unpublished paper.)

Berk, L. E. (1996). Infants, children, and adolescents. Needham Heights, MA: Allyn & Bacon.

Bloom, B. S., Engelhard, M. T., Furst, E. J., Hill, W. H., & Krathwohl, D. R. (1956). Taxonomy of educational objectives: Handbook I: The cognitive domain. New York: David McKay.

California State Department of Education. (1991). Caught in the middle [Films]. Sacramento: Author.

Carnegie Council on Adolescent Development. (1989). Turning points: Preparing American youth for the 21st century. New York: Carnegie Corporation of New York.

Carnegie Council on Adolescent Development. (1995). Great transitions: Preparing adolescents for a new century. New York: Carnegie Corporation of New York.

Cisneros, S. (1991). "Eleven" in Woman Hollering Creek. New York: Vintage Contemporaries.

Dewey, J. (1902). The child and the curriculum. Chicago: University of Chicago Press.

Diaz-Rico, L. T., & Weed, K. Z. (1995). The crosscultural, language, and academic development handbook. Needham Heights, MA: Allyn & Bacon.

Duckworth, E. (1987). The having of wonderful ideas. New York: Columbia University Press.

Erickson, E. (1963). Childhood and society. New York: Norton.

Forman, E. A., Minick, N., & Stone, C. A. (Eds.). (1993). Contexts of learning. London: Oxford University Press.

Garcia, E. (1994). Understanding and meeting the challenge of student cultural diversity. Boston, MA: Houghton Mifflin Co.

George, P. S., & Alexander, W. M. (1993). The exemplary middle school (2nd ed.). Orlando, FL: Harcourt Brace.

George, P. S., & Lawrence, G. (1982). Handbook for middle school teaching. Glenview, Il: Scott Foresman and Company.

George, P. S., & Shewey, K. (1994). New evidence for the middle school. Columbus, OH: National Middle School Association.

Gilligan, C. F. (1982). In a different voice. Cambridge, MA: Harvard University Press.

Goldstein, A. P. (1980). Skill-streaming the adolescent. Champaign, IL: Research Press Co.

Goodlad, J. I. (1979). <u>Curriculum inquiry: The study of curriculum practice</u>. New York: McGraw-Hill.

Goodlad, J. I. (1987). A new look at an old idea: Core curriculum. <u>Educational Leadership</u>, <u>44</u>(4), 8–16.

Harter, P. D., & Gehrke, N. J. (1989). Integrative curriculum: A kaleidoscope of ideas. <u>Educational Horizons, 68</u>(1), 12–17.

International Reading Association and National Council of Teachers of English. (1994). <u>Standards for the assessment of reading and writing.</u> Newark, DE : Author.

Kohlberg, L. (1978). Revisions in the theory and practice of moral development. <u>Moral Development: New Directions for Child Development, 10</u>(2), 83–88.

Lessow-Hurley, J. (1990). <u>The foundations of dual language instruction</u>. New York: Longman.

MacQuiddy, S. L., Maise, S. J., & Hamilton, S. (1987). Empathy and affective perspective taking in parent identified conduct disordered boys. <u>Journal of Clinical and Child Psychology, 16</u>, 260–268.

Manning, M. L. (1994). <u>Celebrating diversity: Multicultural education in middle level schools</u>. Columbus, OH: National Middle School Association.

Marcia, J. E. (1980). Identity in adolescence. In J. Edelson (Ed.), <u>Handbook of adolescent psychology</u> (pp. 159–187). New York: Wiley.

McEwin, C. K., Dickinson, T. S., Erb, T. O., & Scales, P. C. (1995). <u>A vision of excellence: Organizing principles for middle grades teacher preparation</u>. Columbus, OH: National Middle School Association.

Messick, R. G., & Reynolds, K. E. (1992). <u>Middle level curriculum in action</u>. New York: Longman.

Middle Grades Task Force. (1987). <u>Caught in the middle: Educational reform for young adolescents in California public schools</u>. Sacramento: California State Department of Education.

Muth, K. D., & Alvermann, D. E. (1992). <u>Teaching and learning in the middle grades</u>. Boston, MA: Allyn & Bacon.

National Council of Teachers of Mathematics and Mathematical Sciences Educational Board. (1995). <u>Assessment standards for school mathematics</u>. Reston, VA: Author.

National Department of Education. (1995). <u>Digest of Educational Statistics</u>. Washington, DC: Author.

National Middle School Association. (1995). <u>This we believe</u>. Columbus, OH: Author.

National Middle School Association. (Winter, 1995). <u>Target: The newsletter of the National Middle School Association</u>. Columbus, OH: Author.

Office of Technology Assessment. (1992). <u>Report to Congress on the state of technology</u>. Washington, DC: Department of Education.

Phinney, J. S., Chavira, V., & Williamson, L. (1992). The acculturation attitudes and self-esteem among high school and college students. <u>Youth and Society, 23</u>, 299–312.

Rice, F. P. (1995). <u>Human development</u>. Englewood Cliffs, NJ: Prentice-Hall.

Ryan, C. (1994). <u>Authentic assessment</u>. Westminster, CA: Teacher Created Materials.

Scales, P. C. (1992). <u>Windows of opportunity: Improving middle grades teacher preparation</u>. Chapel Hill, NC: Center for Early Adolescence.

Seely, A. (1995). <u>Integrated Thematic Units</u>. Westminster, CA: Teacher Created Materials.

Stevenson, C. (1992). <u>Teaching ten to fourteen-year-olds</u>. New York: Longman.

Stevenson, C., & Carr, J. F. (Eds.). (1993). <u>Integrated studies in the middle grades: Dancing through walls</u>. New York: Teachers College Press.Stiggins, R. J., & Bridgeford, N. J. (1985). The ecology of classroom assessment. <u>Journal of Educational Measurement, (22)</u>, 271–286.

Task Force on Social Studies in the Middle School. (1991). Social studies in the middle school. <u>Social Education, 55,</u> 287–293.

Tatum, B. D. (1992). Talking about race, learning about racism. <u>Harvard Educational Review,</u> <u>62</u>(1), 1–24.

Urdan, T., Midgley, C., & Wood, S. (1995). Special issues in reforming middle level schools. <u>Journal of Early Adolescence, 15</u>(1), 9–37.

Valentine, J. W., Clark, D. C., Irvin, J. I., Keefe, J. W., & Melton, G. (1993). <u>Leadership in middle level education. Volume 1: A national survey of middle level leaders and schools</u>. Reston, VA: National Association of Secondary School Principals.

Vars, G. F. (1961). Organizing instructional materials for teaching core. <u>High School Journal,</u> <u>44</u>(7), 232–238.

Vygotsky, L. (1978). <u>Mind in society</u>. Cambridge, MA: Harvard University Press.